Pan Study Aids

English Language

L. E. W. Smith

Pan Books London and Sydney
in association with **Heinemann Educational Books**

First published 1980 by Pan Books Ltd,
Cavaye Place, London SW10 9PG
in association with Heinemann Educational Books Ltd
   7 8 9
© L. E. W. Smith 1980
ISBN 0 330 25968 7
Printed in Great Britain by
Richard Clay (The Chaucer Press) Ltd, Bungay, Suffolk

Pan Study Aids

Accounts and Book-keeping
Biology
British Government and Politics
Chemistry
Commerce
Economics
Effective Study Skills
English Language
French
Geography 1   *Physical and Human*
Geography 2   *British Isles, Western Europe, North America*
German
History 1   *British*
History 2   *European*
Human Biology
Maths
Physics
Spanish

Advanced Biology
Advanced Chemistry
Advanced Mathematics
Advanced Physics

Brodies Notes on English Literature

This long established series published in Pan Study Aids now contains
more than 150 titles. Each volume covers one of the major works of
English literature regularly set for examinations.

Contents

Acknowledgements

The publishers gratefully acknowledge the permission of the following examining boards, whose addresses are listed on page 6, for the right to reproduce set questions from past examination papers.

Associated Examining Board, University of Cambridge Local Examinations Syndicate, Joint Matriculation Board, Oxford Delegacy of Local Examinations, An Roinn Oideachais, Scottish Certificate of Education Examining Board, University of London School Examinations Department.

The suggested answers to past examination questions are the work of the author and not of the examination boards concerned.

Preface

English Language is the most important of all the examinations. The qualifications for entrance to colleges, banking, nursing, secretarial courses, universities, polytechnics etc., all require O level or equivalent English Language. So a pass in this subject is essential if you are to further your education and career.

English Language is important, however, for another reason. If you are to succeed in any area of life, you need to be able to read with understanding and to express yourself in writing with fluency and clarity. Even in this age of telephones and tapes, the written word is still of primary importance.

There is a further reason why English Language is important. Within the last few years, English has become an international language. Millions of educated people in Europe, North and South America, Africa, Asia and Australasia understand English. So proficiency in English is a 'passport' to this world-wide fellowship of trade, technology, research and other international activities. You need good English for communicating not only in recognized English-speaking countries, but also for nearly every other country of the world.

The aim of this book is to teach you how to make the best use of your own knowledge of English. Every type of question set in the examination is explained, as are the techniques needed to gain good marks in these questions. You can best increase your proficiency in English Language by constant reading, talking, listening and writing. But when you have a good knowledge of English, you must then make the best use of it to pass the examination. That is where this book will prove useful.

L.E.W.S.

The exam boards

The addresses given below are those from which copies of syllabuses and past examination papers may be ordered. The abbreviations (AEB, etc.) are those used in this book to identify actual questions.

Associated Examining Board, (AEB)
Wellington House,
Aldershot, Hants. GU11 1BQ

University of Cambridge Local Examinations Syndicate, (CAM)
Syndicate Buildings, 17 Harvey Road,
Cambridge CB1 2EU

An Roinn Oideachais (ARD)
Department of Education,
Marlborough Street,
Dublin 1

Joint Matriculation Board, (JMB)
(Agent) John Sherratt and Son Ltd.,
78 Park Road,
Altrincham, Cheshire WA14 5QQ

University of London School Examinations Department, (LOND)
66–72 Gower Street,
London WC1E 6EE

Northern Ireland Schools Examinations Council, (NI)
Examinations Office,
Beechill House,
Beechill Road,
Belfast BT8 4RS

Oxford Delegacy of Local Examinations, (OX)
Ewert Place,
Summertown,
Oxford OX2 7BZ

Oxford and Cambridge Schools Examination Board, (O & C)
10 Trumpington Street,
Cambridge CB2 1QB

Scottish Certificate of Education Examining Board, (SCOT)
(Agent) Robert Gibson and Sons, Ltd.,
17 Fitzroy Place,
Glasgow G3 7SF

Southern Universities Joint Board, (SUJB)
Cotham Road, Bristol BS6 6DD

Welsh Joint Education Committee, (WEL)
245 Western Avenue,
Cardiff CF5 2YX

Introduction

This book covers all the English Language syllabuses set by the English O level examination boards, the Scottish, Northern Ireland, Welsh and Irish boards and also the English Language Examination set by the Royal Society of Arts. The papers for all these examining bodies contain questions on composition, comprehension and summary; some also contain additional questions on vocabulary, punctuation and letter-writing: all these questions are covered in this book.

The weighting given to the various questions by the different boards, and within the alternative syllabuses set by some boards, varies considerably. You will need to know which syllabus you are taking, and for which examination board. When you know this you should find out exactly the type of questions you will be expected to answer; how much time you will be given; how many words you will be expected to write for the composition; and how many marks are allowed. You can then concentrate on those sections in this book that are most appropriate to the syllabus you are taking.

The chapters on Composition, Summary and Comprehension are relevant to every syllabus; the chapters on Punctuation and Spelling should be studied by every student because accuracy in these two areas is important in every part of the examination; the chapters on Factual Writing and Vocabulary will be useful to all students, even those whose syllabus does not contain specific questions on these two areas. So the best plan is to read the whole book, then concentrate on the chapters that are most important for your individual needs.

There are two more general points that should be mentioned here. They will be discussed again later, but they are so crucial that you need to grasp their importance from the start.

The first is **timing**. Passing examinations is a question of building up marks and therefore answers not completed because of lack of time, are not awarded any marks. Neither will you be given extra marks because you finished all the questions in half the time allowed. (In fact, you will almost certainly gain less marks than you would have done had you taken all the time allowed!) In other words, you should aim to complete all the questions set, in the time allowed, leaving yourself sufficient time to check over everything you have written to correct all small errors. This means that from the beginning you must train yourself to read the questions, and complete the answers of the length required, in the time allowed. You will then be prepared to complete all the questions in the time allowed in the actual examination, and will retain your accuracy. And you must also leave time to correct your own work, and you must make a habit of doing this.

The second point is related to this. Although your time is limited in the examination, you must always **read all the instructions slowly and carefully**. You will lose marks if you do not do exactly what you are asked to do. Every year, in every examination, dozens of candidates rush into their answers without reading the instructions, and then find they have not done what they should have done. So make a habit of reading thoroughly the instructions to the whole paper and to every question, to make sure you do exactly what you are asked to do – no more, and no less. You will then give yourself a much better chance of passing this examination.

1 Composition

The most important question in the English Language Examination is the composition. Sometimes the question is called 'essay', or 'continuous writing', but the various names are not important as they all amount to the same thing: you are asked to write a piece of prose of about two to three pages. Because it is so important one board even asks for two compositions, and in nearly every English Language examination the marks given for the composition are higher than for any other single question.

One thing should be made clear from the beginning: this question aims to test your ability to write well-organized, clear, precise and accurate English. It is not a test in creative writing or imagination. The examiners are not looking for budding Graham Greenes or Isaac Asimovs. The examiners want to see that you can punctuate, spell and paragraph correctly; that you can write good and varied sentences; and that your composition is well planned and well laid-out. Even the most creative, imaginative, original story will be awarded a very low mark if it contains bad spelling, punctuation and paragraphing. A straightforward, unoriginal composition with correct spelling, paragraphing and punctuation, and which is well-organized and planned, will gain a good mark, though not the highest mark. There is no sense in complaining about this. If you want to pass O level English, you must do what the syllabus asks you to do.

Every syllabus has instructions that can be summarized as follows:

1 Plan your composition carefully.
2 Divide your composition into paragraphs, with an introduction and conclusion, and with appropriate emphasis and sequence of ideas.
3 Take care with grammar, spelling and punctuation.
4 Write in a style appropriate to the nature of the material and the form

of your composition (narrative, descriptive, discursive, dramatic etc.).
5 Marks are given for good English and orderly presentation.
6 Work is assessed on quality and not quantity (so long as the composition is of the minimum length required).

We will look at these points in detail later on in this chapter, but first let us look at the timing for this question.

The time allowed for the composition varies from 50 minutes to one hour. Find out how much time is allowed by the board whose paper you are taking, and practise writing essays in that time. There is no sense in allowing yourself to write much longer, or shorter essays in the preparation period; you will then find it difficult to readjust yourself for the actual examination. It is far better, from the beginning, to have allowed yourself the same time as you will have in the examination, and write essays of the length required.

If the time allowed is one hour, that time should be divided as follows:

1 1 or 2 minutes to read through the instructions to the paper, slowly and carefully, to make sure you do exactly what you are asked to do. Never rush straight on to the questions. There is plenty of time, so long as you take things in an organized way. And there is nothing worse in an examination than not doing what you are asked to do. So make sure you understand the instructions at the top of the paper.
2 3 or 4 minutes to read through all the questions and choose the topic for your composition.
3 10–15 minutes to plan your composition.
4 About 40 minutes to write your composition, which should give you plenty of time to write, neatly and clearly, the two or three pages required.
5 5 minutes to read over what you have written to correct all the small errors.

(If your time is less or more than one hour, it is the time allowed for the writing which will vary most, as you will be expected to hand in a composition of a slightly different length.)

So the main divisions of time for the composition paper are:

1 Reading the instructions
2 Choice
3 Plan

4 The writing
5 Re-reading and correcting.

We will consider each of these in turn. But first, let us look at a typical exam paper. This one allows one hour for the composition, but this can vary with different boards and you should check the time that your board allows.

English Language
Ordinary Level

COMPOSITION

Time: one hour
Write on one of the following. Pay careful attention to spelling, punctuation and handwriting.

1 *Telepathy.*
2 *The view from the top of a hill.*
3 *Describe a visit you have made to some place of interest. (It could be a museum, exhibition, theatre, factory, archaeological site etc.)*
4 *Write a story for which the following is the last sentence:*
  He never did know what it was he should have brought back.
5 *What are the advantages and disadvantages of television?*
6 *Two friends have had a misunderstanding. Set the scene, and then write a conversation between the two friends in which the misunderstanding is cleared up.*
7 *What do the following lines bring to your mind?*
  'Did you ever dream when you were young
  Of floating through the air, hung
  Between the clouds and the gay
  Be-blossomed land?'
8 *Write a composition based on the accompanying photograph.*

Choice
This brings you to the first difficulty. How do you choose the subject for your composition?

First, note how the questions ask for different kinds of writing. For example, which of the compositions above would be descriptive, narrative, discursive, conversational or impressionistic? During your preparation for this question, you should find out what kinds of writing suit you best. It is better to be versatile and not to restrict yourself to one type – it might not appear on the examination paper.

Secondly, ask yourself which topic gives you the opportunity to write a full and interesting composition. Although this is not a test in creative writing, you will nevertheless gain the highest marks only if your material is correct, lively and interesting. The best writing comes from first-hand experience moulded by imagination. So you must ask yourself which topic interests you particularly. Have you first-hand experience of any of them?

Let us consider each of the eight topics in turn, and consider the kind of writing that is asked for.

1 Telepathy

One-word titles are always difficult, as they allow such a wide choice of treatment. This could, for example, be treated as a straightforward essay on telepathy, giving the scientific evidence for and against it. (This requires a discursive treatment.) Or it could be a general-interest essay giving examples of telepathy you have experienced. (This could be partly descriptive, partly narrative, and partly discursive.) Or you could treat it as a narrative (or story) in which telepathy plays a major part, and for which 'Telepathy' provides a suitable title. Only tackle a discursive composition if you have studied and know the subject.

You would be unwise to tackle either the general-interest composition, or the narrative, unless you have had some first-hand experience of telepathy. Here again it would be all too easy to wander from the topic, or to dry up for want of interesting material.

2 The view from the top of a hill

This is obviously a descriptive composition, and one which anybody could write. But you would be unwise to attempt this question unless you did know, at first-hand, a particular view from a particular hill. What you write need not be factually true (this is not an examination in fact, so you can mould your material as much as you like to make a good composition), but your writing would most likely be stale and lifeless if it were not based on your own experience.

This is one of the questions we will plan and write later in this chapter, so we will leave further discussion until then (pp 18–20).

3 Describe a visit you have made to some place of interest. (It could be a museum, exhibition, theatre, factory, archaeological site etc.)

Here again, this is a descriptive piece of writing, and again you would be unwise to choose it unless you had recently visited some place of interest.

If you had, and you found the visit exciting, then your writing would reflect this in its style.

But there are two particular dangers with this type of composition, and they are both concerned with the organization and planning.

The first danger is that with this type of subject, it is all too easy to spend about half the composition before you arrive at the 'place of interest'. The topic you are asked to write on is the *place of interest*; not how you got there. Of course, how and why you went to the place can provide a good introduction, and your thoughts when you came away a good conclusion – but they must both be kept brief and in proportion.

The second danger concerns the appropriate emphasis in your composition. Your answer should consist of an introduction, then four, five or six paragraphs (according to the length of composition you are asked to write), then a conclusion. The middle paragraphs should be of roughly equal length and interest. Now when you go to a place of interest, there is very often one thing that particularly captures your attention; this is the danger for your composition: you can all too easily concentrate on this one thing in one long, interesting paragraph, then dismiss all the rest in three or four short and uninteresting paragraphs. Your composition would be badly proportioned. This is where you must use your imagination to mould your material into a well-planned piece of writing.

4 *Write a story for which the following is the last sentence: He never did know what it was he should have brought back.*

This is obviously narrative – a short story. 'Creative writing', you might say and this is the danger. Although it is, undoubtedly, creative, the examiners are still looking for accurate spelling, punctuation, paragraphing, sentence structure and grammar. A lively and ingenious story will gain a good mark only if it has this mechanical accuracy.

Another problem is that, unless you are good at it, it is very difficult to write a good story in the 'two or three pages' allowed by the syllabus. It is not easy to establish the scene and the characters in that short space. Even professional writers find this difficult. It is all too easy to ramble on in an uninteresting and inconsequential way before arriving at that final sentence. It is very easy, as well, to write too much, and so leave yourself insufficient time to correct your work carefully. A short story among the questions should not be seen as an opportunity for a display of creativity; to gain a good mark, your story will need good organization, strict discipline, and careful attention to all details. A good narrative should contain a logical sequence of events, leading to a good conclusion.

5 What are the advantages and disadvantages of televison?
This is the discursive topic, giving the opportunity for well-organized argument. There is usually at least one question which allows for this kind of writing. One thing to watch with this type of question is that it usually asks for *advantages and disadvantages*; in other words, you have to balance both sides of the discussion. The topics set are often ones on which you are likely to have strong opinions, and the danger is to write giving only one point of view, not balancing it against the other view. So don't rush into a question that gives you the opportunity to ride your pet hobby-horse without carefully considering exactly what you are asked to do.

A plan for this essay will be given later in this chapter (pp 20–2).

If you do like debate and argument, this is a good question to tackle. It is possible, in the space of two or three pages, to write a neatly balanced discussion on a controversial topic, leading in with a short general introduction, and then, in the conclusion, either coming down on one side or the other, or indeed leaving the question open. The discursive question is one for those with a thoughtful and logical mind.

6 Two friends have had a misunderstanding. Set the scene, and then write a conversation between the two friends in which the misunderstanding is cleared up.
Most of this composition is going to be conversation, or direct speech. Direct speech needs more attention to the details of punctuation than does any other form of writing (see p 147). So you would be unwise to tackle a question like this unless you are good at punctuation; you can lose so many marks even before you have started.

Generally speaking, it is unwise to use slang expressions in a composition in the O level examination, but in a conversation between friends you would have to use the kind of tone and speech used between people who know each other well. However, *don't overdo it*. Moderation and restraint are more likely to impress the examiner than is your knowledge of all the latest swear-words.

A composition like this is a difficult one to plan. It needs thought and careful attention if it is not to degenerate into inconsequential ramblings.

7 *What do the following lines bring to your mind?*
> 'Did you ever dream when you were young
> Of floating through the air, hung
> Between the clouds and the gay
> Be-blossomed land?'

This kind of open question, with a few evocative lines from a poem, is a favourite of both examining boards and candidates. But, unless you are very wary, it can be a trap question. Once again, it is all too easy to fall into a disorganized display of creativity.

A question such as 'What do the following lines bring to your mind?' is an invitation for an impressionistic piece of writing, because there is no telling what two or three lines of verse do bring to your mind. They could bring something completely irrelevant to the quotation; one word in the lines could have a peculiar meaning which blots out the real sense.

Do remember, once again, that you are writing a composition for an O level English Language examination. The examiners are looking for good English and orderly presentation. So, for the purposes of the examination it is better to mould your thoughts into a well-planned composition which has close relevance to the sense of the quotation. (The poem from which the quotation comes is about parachuting.) It should have a good, short introduction that leads into your impressions (or story, or description), and be rounded off with a short conclusion. (A plan for this essay is given on p 23.)

8 *Write a composition based on the accompanying photograph.*
The 'visual stimulus' technique is another favourite of both examination boards and candidates. With your examination paper you are given one or two photographs or drawings, and then asked to write on one of them. No photograph is given here; but it is usually something evocative, or humorous, or controversial.

The dangers are similar to those in a question giving a few lines of verse; it is all too easy to wander too far from what is actually in the drawing or photograph. You must look at it very closely, and in detail; often there is one particularly telling detail, and if you miss that, you miss the whole point of the picture. And you must make sure that everything you write is relevant to the picture, and is well-organized and presented.

This kind of question is regarded by many candidates as an easy option because they don't have to use their imagination too much. All the details are 'visualized' for you. But 'easy options' are generally to be avoided in examinations; they don't draw the best out of you. So if you do choose to write on the 'visual stimulus', remember it is not the easy option.

This discussion of a set of typical examination topics should enable you to see the kind of questions you should be asking yourself when you receive your examination paper. If you consider the variety of questions *now*, you should be able to make up your mind much faster on the actual examination day.

So when you go into the examination room don't waste time glancing round at your friends or silently cursing your luck. You are in to pass this paper, so get down to it straightaway. You have no time to waste.

Read through the instructions at the head of the paper. Then, slowly and carefully, read through the subjects set. Then read them through again. Some will probably cancel themselves out, and you will probably be left with two or three possibles.

Select the one which interests you most, the one which excites you, or the one which will give you the opportunity to use your own particular talent. Your work before the examination should have pointed to your particular skills.

When you have made your choice, write the title at the head of a piece of rough paper. Forget all the others. This is the subject of your composition and you must concentrate your energies on that alone. Remember that what the examiners are looking for is good English, and not information. Your subject-matter should be relevant and interesting, but it is the way that it is organized and expressed that is important in this examination.

Having made your choice within the first 3 or 4 minutes, you are ready to make your plan.

Plan

The next 10 minutes will probably decide whether you are going to pass this paper or not. It is precisely because your time is limited that you must spend at least 10 minutes planning what you are going to write. Otherwise your effort will be purposeless and shapeless; you will dry up in the middle; or you will wander from the set subject.

As ideas come into your mind, jot them down, as roughly as you like, and as many as you can in 4 or 5 minutes. This is your raw material which must be sorted out to make a composition.

For some people, however, this is precisely where the trouble starts. Ideas do not come into their mind and the piece of paper remains blank.

How can you induce a flow of ideas? Here are some suggestions to help you.

1 Make your thinking on the topic personal rather than general. For example, if the subject is 'Trees', don't try to think of all the different varieties of trees in the world; concentrate your thoughts on one or two particular trees or woods that you know. Think about a time when you were standing under them. Or make a start at a sawmill you know, with its sounds and scents. As soon as you have a particular personal starting point, especially if you can recall the sights, sounds, feel and smell, the ideas begin to flow.

2 Make your thinking definite. If your topic is a general one, such as 'Saturday Jobs', don't try to think vaguely about the pros and cons, but start your thinking with precise and definite jobs such as working in a supermarket, or as a garage attendant, preferably based on your own experience or that of a close friend.

3 Direct your thinking into examples which have really affected you deeply, either pleasurably or painfully. You are then much more likely to become involved in your subject. Then your reader will also become involved, and share your pleasure or pain.

4 When you do begin to feel involved, and associations begin to come into your mind, jot down definite examples, even if at first they seem irrelevant. These examples can spark off further ideas which are relevant, and then, in your plan, you can miss out the first irrelevant material. But they have served as a catalyst to precipitate the material you do want.

5 When ideas start to flow, elaborate and supplement them with your own personal interests, experience and knowledge. For example, the person who planned the essay which is discussed on the next few pages, 'The view from the top of a hill', was obviously interested in history, so the ideas are held together and elaborated with historical associations. If your particular interest were hang-gliding, your personal interests, experience and knowledge of 'The view from the top of a hill' would be quite different, and you should use them.

6 What you should always remember is that none of us share the same flow of ideas, images, pictures, or associations. It is this unique, personal experience which should make the raw material of your composition.

From your raw material select one line of thought which you can follow through in the space of five or six paragraphs. Each paragraph will treat of one aspect of your subject. Your paragraphs must follow logically one from the other, so on your rough plan superimpose 1, 2, 3, 4, 5 – depending on the number of paragraphs you require – to show which ideas are going into each paragraph. Some ideas can often be linked together. Some will need to be supplemented with additional material. Remember that correct spelling, punctuation and grammar will not gain you a high mark if your essay is dull and lifeless. It is while you are planning that you should muster your resources to make your essay interesting and alive by bringing in first-hand observation, examples and information which are relevant to your subject. Add them to your plan with their appropriate paragraph numbers. Cross out all the material you are not going to use: it might distract you from your main purpose.

We will imagine that from our selection of subjects the only essay we could tackle is the one on 'The View from the Top of a Hill'. This is the kind of composition which anybody could write (there is usually one such title in every selection) but that is no reason why the essay should be uninteresting. On a piece of rough paper we wrote our title and then jotted down the thoughts as they came:

The view from the top of a hill
Peak Hill – river – river mouth – town in distance with smoke haze – the coastline with cliff-falls – sitting on mound on top of hill – Iron-Age fort – where the Saxon raiders landed? – imagine what the hill has seen – peaceful commerce – war and raids – the peaceful countryside – what has changed? – what is likely to change? – atomic power station just down coast – the steep climb up the hill – difficult to attack – the approach through narrow lanes – sun shining on chalk cliffs to east – flints from chalk – Stone-Age axes from this hill in British Museum – France over sea to south – different colours on sea – wind and deep water – sea air makes you hungry – estuary to west where Romans probably exported lead and silver – inland, another fort in distance commanding valley – fire beacons – news of Trafalgar.

This is the raw material from which our composition must be constructed. We need not use everything, and we can incorporate new ideas as the plan takes shape. We have found from practice that an essay of five or six paragraphs is the best length. (This is for one hour. You should decide, while you are practising writing essays in the time allowed by your examination board, how many paragraphs you need.)

An introduction immediately suggests itself – 'the steep climb up the hill'. We put 1 against this on our rough plan. It will have to be filled out when we come to write the introduction. (*NB* We could have introduced our essay by 'the approach to the hill through narrow lanes', but this would have started too far away from 'The View from the Top of a Hill'. This is a common fault: the subject is approached by such devious ways that a page or more has been written before the composition comes to the point.)

A conclusion is suggested by 'sea air makes you hungry', so we put 6 against this. 'The wind over the sea' will lead naturally to an appetite, and so to the scramble down the hill to find a café for tea.

The most obvious arrangement for the four middle paragraphs would be the view when facing east, south, west and north, giving one paragraph for each direction, and there is no reason why such a mechanical organization should lead to a dull essay. The raw material, however, seems to need a more spontaneous treatment.

The view from Peak Hill is obviously rich with historical associations, and these should be taken into account in our plan. We could arrange our material chronologically: Stone Age, Roman, Saxon, Modern. But this type of essay nearly always lapses into dullness. Far too many essays on 'Ships', for example, begin with dug-out canoes and inevitably progress through galleons and steamships to atomic submarines. There is not the space in a six-paragraph essay to write an interesting pocket history on any subject. Unless the topic specifically invites it, the chronological approach should be avoided.

How, then, are we to arrange our material?

Using the historical associations we can range from one aspect of the view to another, just as if two friends were pointing out the landmarks to each other and making comments of interest. Such an approach could move freely through time and space, all the material being brought together by being part of 'The View from the Top of a Hill'.

This would be the paragraph arrangement of the essay:

Introduction: steep climb up hill – view worth the effort – sea to south – coastline – hill the highest point – sitting on mound.
Paragraph 2: part of Iron-Age fort – must have been difficult to attack– flints for axes and arrowheads came from chalk cliffs to east where sun is shining – in the distance, another fort, inland, commanding the valley – called Beacon Hill – news travelled by fire beacons.
Paragraph 3: imagine what this hill has seen – this coast is where

Saxon raiders probably landed – river mouth good landing place – see inland along valley – town in distance with smoke haze – Roman road near town.

Paragraph 4: that road still leads to estuary to west – where Romans exported lead and silver – near where atomic power station being built – cranes along the river edge.

Paragraph 5: what has changed? – countryside much the same – cliff-falls indication that coastline has changed – this fort much further inland when my Stone-Age counterpart sat on this mound – sea, in its ever-changing moods, still unchanged – different colours – effects of deeper water and wind.

Conclusion: sea air makes you hungry – leave view and its memories – scramble down steep slope to find café for tea.

Notes on this plan

1 The last idea of each paragraph is connected with the first idea in the next, so that the links between the paragraphs can be made easily and naturally.
2 The conclusion, coming back to the steepness of the slope which was mentioned in the introduction, should round off the composition satisfactorily.
3 We must make sure that each idea is related to the subject, 'The View from the Top of a Hill'. The Stone-Age axes in the British Museum, although interesting, must be omitted as they are not relevant to the subject. (Here we could erect a danger signal: beware of dragging in irrelevant material.) The Roman road at the end of the third paragraph can be associated with the subject because we can say that we can still see the course of that road.
4 This plan is based on a view that the author knows well, but the details are freely adapted. You should always base your writings on your personal experience, writing on what you know rather than what you've learned from books or acquired from television or other sources. First-hand observation, sincerely expressed, usually comes alive for the reader. You can mould the facts to suit your purpose, and you can supplement your material with acquired knowledge, but the basis of all your writing should be something which has happened to you, and not second-hand information.

Let us look now at the plan for a different kind of composition, the discursive essay. We will choose the topic given earlier in this chapter as our example:

5 What are the advantages and disadvantages of television?

It is important in a composition of this type to have a well-developed, logical argument (or line of thought), and a good balance between the advantages and the disadvantages. Once again, we will plan for an introduction and a conclusion and four main paragraphs.

Each paragraph will discuss one aspect of the main topic. This, in fact, is what a paragraph is: a smaller unit (usually of about four or five sentences in an essay of this length), which deals with one aspect of the main subject.

With the discursive essay you need to decide which aspects of the topic you are going to discuss in each paragraph. It is not enough to jot down random ideas as they come into your mind, as you can for a descriptive or impressionistic composition; you need to direct your thoughts to make sure you are including important points.

Here your main points could be: education, news, sport and entertainment. These are the main topics of the four middle paragraphs. You then need to decide in which order to discuss them. It is usually better to put the least important first, and work up to the most important last; this means that your composition should work up to a strong conclusion, and not fizzle out weakly. In fact, this is a good general rule when planning an essay: keep the most interesting and important point until the end. Here we decide to discuss the four main points in the following order:

1 Entertainment;   2 Sport;   3 News;   4 Education.

Your plan could look like this:

Introduction: recent spread of television satellites enables programmes to be seen simultaneously all over the world – what will be the effect of this?

Entertainment

For: provides relaxation – some programmes well-produced, witty and amusing – serialization of classics stimulates people to read.

Against: people once provided their own entertainment, now just watchers – far too much violence in many programmes.

Sport

For: enables people all over the world to see international events such as Olympic Games and World Cup as they actually happen – brings people of the world together – makes young people want to participate.

Against: because nations are 'on show' too much nationalism is brought into sport – national prestige and not sportsmanship becomes of prime importance – some nations do anything (drugs) to win.

News
For: people all over the world can see what is happening – this promotes a 'world consciousness', and gives all people comparisons with their own conditions.
Against: emphasis on violence or disasters – terrorists get world-wide publicity – news is censored in many countries, so a true picture is not given.

Education
For: not only educational programmes, but many documentaries mean people are much better informed – new horizons opened.
Against: programmes can become propaganda – people are either misled, or their expectations are raised too high – if all people sought 'western' standards, disastrous effect on world's resources – does all this knowledge make people any wiser?

Conclusion: The phenomenon of television is too new to judge as yet what the results will be – but the world will never be the same – too early to say if it is a force for good or evil.

To make the line of argument clear, this plan is filled out more fully than you would need to do in the examination. One or two words in each section would be enough to remind you of your argument and examples. What you should realize is that with a more formal essay, you need to plan in a more formal way. You need a clear, well-balanced plan to enable you to write a clear, well-balanced essay. It is the consideration of 'appropriate emphasis' that can best be accounted for at the planning stage.

With a narrative (or story), your plan should ensure that one event follows easily and logically on from the one before. Each event in the main story should have a separate paragraph. There is, however, one important point to note here: if you include direct speech (or conversation) in your story, then each new speaker must have a new paragraph. (See p 149.) But even so, your plan should list the main sequence of events, and any conversation that comes into any of these events should be seen as technical paragraphing within the main paragraph (or plan) structure. And don't forget that a narrative also needs a good introduction to the story, and also a good rounding off or conclusion. It mustn't just tail off at the end.

The conversational composition must also be planned if it is not to wander inconsequentially. You need to have a good introduction which sets the scene and introduces the speakers, then decide on the four or five areas of interest that are going to be covered in the conversation, leading to a good conclusion. But although your plan will show four or five areas to be covered, there will be many more paragraphs, because every new speaker must have a new paragraph. Here again, it is really technical paragraphing within a longer paragraph plan.

The impressionistic composition, particularly one based on a few lines of a poem or on a photograph or drawing, is one of the most difficult to control. Sometimes, in an inspired moment, you might be able to write a well-shaped composition without any planning. But it is dangerous to risk this in the examination; inspiration tends to dry up when you are under the pressure of an examination. It is far safer to attempt an essay based on a poem or picture in an orderly way. You can then keep control of yourself and your writing. So the plan of the composition based on the poem in the selection given earlier, could go as follows.

Let us first remind ourselves of the question:

7   *What do the following lines bring to your mind?*
   'Did you ever dream when you were young
   Of floating through the air, hung
   Between the clouds and the gay
   Be-blossomed land?'

Introduction: Dreams about flying common – children also daydream about being a bird.
Paragraph 2: Man has always wanted to fly – gods and mythological creatures (angels) could fly – man earthbound.
Paragraph 3: Now we can fly – great speeds and distances, but also noisy and claustrophobic – like being in a bus.
Paragraph 4: Glider or parachuting nearer to the childhood dream – just the sound of the wind – time to admire the earth below.
Paragraph 5: But not the same thing as being able to float about in the air – the earth looks 'gay' and 'be-blossomed' in childhood – always springtime.
Conclusion: The trouble is we wake up from the dream when we grow up – it is autumn not spring – the ground muddy.

Many students resist the making of a plan. Some say they make a plan in their head; but it is very easy to forget it when under the pressure of an actual examination. Some say a plan inhibits their style so they cannot get a free flow of ideas; but ideas do not flow so easily in the examination room. Some say that there is only one hour to write the composition so there is no time to make a plan; but it is precisely because the time is so limited that you are advised to make a plan; if you do not, you are much more likely to wander from the subject set, or to dry up in the middle. The choice, of course, is yours; but all experience shows that for a vast majority of candidates, it is far better to spend those 10–15 minutes planning what you are going to write.

The writing

When you are practising the writing of compositions, from the very beginning try to make them the same length as will be required in the examination. Most boards say '2 to 3 sides of examination paper of average-size handwriting'. A good average length is 500 words. Only two boards actually suggest less than this (Oxford and Cambridge give '350–500 words' and London 'not less than 450 words'), and only one specifies more (Welsh Board gives 500–600 words). So count up how many words, on average, you write to a line, and then see how many lines make 500 words in the kind of exercise book or file you normally use. Most examination boards now use examination books for answers, and the size of the sheets of paper is often considerably larger than the average-size exercise book. You should also time how long it takes you to write 500 words, neatly and clearly; most people can easily write 500 words within 30 minutes.

The most difficult paragraph to write is the introduction. You should try to claim your reader's attention and then focus it on the line of thought you plan to develop. Beware of making your introduction too long: three or four sentences are usually sufficient.

The most important sentence is the first. The first thought which comes into your head is rarely the best. Do not, for example, begin a composition on 'Messages' with the sentence: 'There are many different ways of sending messages.' This is so obvious that it is not worth saying. Make your first sentence short and thought-provoking. The first words of 'Messages', for example, could be 'Mayday! Mayday!' That, at least, is far more arresting.

Don't forget to indent the first word of each new paragraph at least one inch from the margin. Make a habit of doing this always. It helps your reader to see quite clearly where each new paragraph starts, and so to follow the development of your plan. And then make sure all other lines begin close to the margin, so that the left-hand side of your page is neat, like print in a book.

Help your reader to follow the line of thought in your essay by providing phrases which link your paragraphs together. For example, in an essay which is presenting different views on some subject, having given one side of the question in one paragraph, you could begin your next paragraph with the phrase, 'On the other hand . . .', or 'In spite of this . . .', depending on your argument; the last paragraph could then begin with a phrase such as 'For these reasons . . .'.

This concluding paragraph is almost as difficult to write as the introduction. It should give the reader the satisfying feeling of completeness. If your last word happened to coincide with the end of the last line on a page, the reader should feel that there is no need to turn over. You can often achieve this effect by using some phrase or idea that you have used in the introduction.

Write easily and naturally; write, within polite limits, what you honestly think and feel, and not what you imagine the examiner wants you to write. You should have plenty of time to keep your writing neat and your paragraphing tidy. Examiners are human, and an examiner who is annoyed and insulted through having to mark almost illegible writing, is bound to give a lower mark.

Here is how the two compositions that we have planned in detail in this chapter, could be written out in full. Always remember to put the question number in the margin, especially if you do not write out the title. Otherwise it is not always clear to the examiner which question you are answering.

First turn back to pp 19–20 and re-read the plan for the first composition, and the notes about it. You can then follow how the plan is transcribed into the completed essay.

---

2 The view from the top of a hill

It is a steep climb up Peak Hill, but the view from the top is worth the effort. To the south is the sea, with the coastline stretching east and west. This is the highest point for miles around, so the sea and the country inland are laid out below. To enjoy the view, I am sitting on a mound at the very top of the hill.

This earthwork is part of an Iron-Age fort. It must have been very difficult to attack, even when defended with primitive weapons. To the east, along the coast, the sun is shining on the chalk cliffs where the flints came from to make the axes and arrowheads that are still often found here. Inland, too, is another fort, still called Beacon Hill, a reminder of the time when important news travelled by fire beacons.

What history has the hill seen? This coast is one place where the Saxons invaded. The river mouth just to the west, where the sun is glinting, would make a safe harbour; and then the raiders could penetrate along the valley towards the town in the distance. All I can see of the town now is a slight smoke haze, but threading straight over the hills I can make out the line of the Roman road that still gives that town its name.

Part of that road is now the foundation for the motorway that leads to the estuary. I can hear the hum of the traffic, even though the cars and lorries look no bigger than insects. Occasionally a windscreen flashes in the sun like a signal of a new age. In their day, the Romans exported lead and silver from very near the spot where now a new atomic power station is being built. I can just see the giant cranes, standing up at the water's edge like mechanical dinosaurs.

What, I wonder, has changed since my Stone-Age counterpart sat on this mound? The contours of the hills and valleys inland were much the same, although there was probably then much more forest, and not the patchwork of fields and hedgerows I can see now. The fresh red earth of the new cliff-falls stands out in the sun; but it is a reminder that the coastline has been changing all the time. This fort must have been much further inland when it was built, but even then with a view over the sea. In fact, the sea itself, with its ever-changing moods, is the one thing that has not changed at all. Since time began, the waves breaking on the shingle have been making the sound I can hear now. People of all ages, as they sat here, must have marvelled at the different shades of blue and green, the effects of deeper water and currents, and the patterns the wind makes on the waves.

The wind over the sea, with its salty tang, must also have made anyone who sat here feel hungry. I realize I am. I must leave the view with its rich legacy of memories. Now for the scramble back down this steep slope! I know the farmer's wife in that old farmhouse I can see nestling in the trees at the bottom, serves very good cream teas.

Points to note about this composition
1 It is just over 500 words, the right length for any examining board.
2 With this length of composition there is space to develop only four or five subsidiary ideas. This means four or five paragraphs – not counting the introduction and conclusion.

3 The paragraphs are of roughly equal length, and it is quite clear where each new paragraph begins. You need about four, five or six sentences to develop the theme of each paragraph.

4 The sentences are varied. For example, the first sentence of the second paragraph is a simple sentence; but the next three sentences in that paragraph are all complex sentences. This gives variety. Study the sentence structure of the other paragraphs.

5 The first sentence of each new paragraph makes a link with the preceding paragraph. For example, the 'earthwork' mentioned in the first sentence of the second paragraph links with the 'mound' in the last sentence of the introduction. Find the link words or ideas between the other paragraphs.

6 The composition begins by mentioning the steepness of the climb up; in the last paragraph we come back to the steep slope down. This has the effect of rounding off the composition.

7 Although the composition is about the view, so it is chiefly about things seen, there are two images which give sounds: 'the hum of the traffic on the motorway', and 'the waves on the shingle'. (This is justified here because one feature of being on top of a hill is the clarity with which sounds can be heard.) There is also one image involving scent: 'the salty tang of the wind from the sea'. There is an important lesson to learn here. Writing becomes more vivid when all the senses are involved, so try to bring in images of scent, touch, sound and taste, as well as sight. Your reader can then more vividly imagine what you are describing because it affects all his senses. It means that you too must imagine the whole scene more vividly.

8 All the spelling is correct, and all the punctuation marks are in the correct places. Notice, particularly, the two question marks; they are very often forgotten by careless candidates. Notice the way that a few sentences make use of semi-colons. There is one exclamation mark too.

9 There is no attempt to show off by using long words or elaborate similes or metaphors. This composition might not gain full marks, but it would get a very good grade.

We will now turn to the discursive essay, and complete that. First turn back to p 21 and re-read the plan.

---

5 *What are the advantages and disadvantages of television?*
The World Cup Final was watched by half the population of the world. The use of satellites has enabled any television programme to

be seen simultaneously all over the world. Never before have people been able to see what is happening on the other side of the Earth – or the Moon – as it actually happens. What effect will this have on the people of the world?

For one thing, millions of people will be entertained. Many television programmes are well-produced, witty and amusing, and they provide good relaxation. However, many programmes also contain far too much violence, so children grow up accepting shooting and thuggery as the norm. In the old days, too, people made their own entertainments; now they are just box-watchers, a passive audience instead of active participants. But, on the other hand, when a classic serial is televized, the libraries and bookshops immediately have a new demand for that book; people want to read it for themselves.

A similar phenomenon happens with sport. Television now enables people all over the world to see international sporting events, such as the Olympic Games or the World Cup, as they actually happen. This brings the people of the world together; they are all part of the same audience. And when young people see so much sport, they themselves want to participate. But when nations are 'on view', national prestige and not individual sportsmanship becomes of prime importance. Some nations are willing to indulge in most unscrupulous tactics, such as administering dangerous drugs, so long as they see their flag raised at the victory ceremony. Sport is used, because of its impact on television, to raise the nation's morale.

Terrorist organizations have also been quick to realize the impact of television. Through the news programmes, people can now see what is happening all over the world, and this promotes a 'world consciousness', and also enables people to make comparisons with their own conditions. But because violence and disasters are the most newsworthy items, an unbalanced picture is given of what is happening. Furthermore, by actually causing violence and disasters, terrorists can ensure they get world-wide publicity for their cause. It must also be remembered, too, that every televized programme is 'edited', so it is all too easy to censor or slant the news, so that people can be manipulated when they think they are watching 'the truth'.

Governments can also similarly control their education programmes. Television is a potent force for propaganda. But there is no doubt that millions more people are much better informed. Not only actual educational programmes, but many documentaries open out new horizons. But will this raise people's expectations too high? If everyone in the

world sought standards of living similar to that in the 'West', it could
have a disastrous effect on the limited natural resources of the Earth.
And, anyway does all this knowledge make people any wiser?

Television is too new to say what its effect will be. Is it a force for good
or evil? One thing is clear: the world will never be the same again.
Because of television, we now live on a much smaller planet.

Points to note about this composition.

1 It is just 500 words; the right length for any examining board.
2 Within such a limited space, the case *for* and *against* must be very
   closely argued. Everything is to the point, and there is no irrelevant
   digression.
3 The links between the paragraphs are made (trace them yourself)
   to develop the argument from one paragraph to the next. Within the
   paragraphs themselves, words and phrases such as 'however',
   'but', 'on the other hand', make the contrast between the good and
   bad aspects of television.
4 The paragraphs are of roughly equal length, so all four topics –
   entertainment, sport, news, education – have equal emphasis. Within
   the paragraphs themselves, the points *for* and *against* are given just
   about equal weight. Note how they are not given mechanically –
   for in the first half of the paragraph and *against* in the second –
   but are merged in a natural flow, although both sides are kept clear.
5 The conclusion comes back to the point that was raised in the
   introduction – the effect of television on the people of the world. This
   rounds off the composition. It doesn't come to any conclusion, in the
   sense of proving anything, but there is no need for the conclusion
   of a composition to do that. You are not doing a sum that must have a
   correct answer. Very often, having compared both sides, it is
   better to leave the question open, as here.
6 A good vocabulary is needed to write a good discursive composition.
   There are many useful words used here that you would do well to
   add to your vocabulary.

Re-reading and correcting

We come now to the last 5 minutes of the time allowed for the composition – minutes which can gain you many marks.

Everyone, particularly when writing under stress, makes small errors
of punctuation, or spelling, or missing out small words, or just careless-
ness. If you hand in your work without correcting all these small errors

you will lose many marks. That is foolish, because you could have saved these marks.

So you must leave yourself at least 5 minutes to read over what you have written, and **neatly** and **clearly**, correct any mistakes. Any word misspelt should be neatly crossed out, and the correct spelling written legibly over the top. Any alteration which cannot be clearly read, or is ambiguous, is counted as wrong. So all corrections must be clear; otherwise they are still wrong.

You must train yourself to correct your own work, and you must start your training from the very beginning. Many people read over their work, giving themselves a pat on the back, and miss all the mistakes. This is useless. Re-read your work as if it were written by someone else, looking for the errors. The most common mistakes are: question marks missed out; the full-stop omitted at the ends of paragraphs or at the very end; inverted commas left out at the end of speech; apostrophes missed out; *it's* confused with *its*.

Professional writers, before their book is printed, have to proof-read every page to make sure there are no mistakes. (Have you found any in this book?) Train yourself to be a good proof-reader of your own work. It will save you many marks.

Examination practice

1 Plan two more of the compositions given on p 11.

2 Write one of the compositions you have planned.

3 Plan and write three further compositions from the following:

   (a) Trees.

   (b) A knock on the door.

   (c) 'Men and women never will be equal.' What are your views on this topic?

   (d) Write a story in which a dog, or a cat, or a horse, plays an important part.

   (e) A person who left your district many years ago is revisiting it for the first time. Write a conversation between this person, and someone who has lived there all the time, discussing the changes that have taken place.

   (f) Find a photograph or drawing that interests you, and then write a story, or description, or composition based on it.

   (g) Write a short play in which two friends quarrel, and then make up. Set the scene in the stage directions.

2 Factual Writing (including letter-writing)

All examining boards include an essay in their papers. About half of them also include an additional exercise in composition, usually not more than one page long. This is set to test your ability to write clear, accurate and well-organized prose. As one board put it on one of its examination papers: 'You should understand that this question is designed to test your accuracy in the writing of English and in your use of the material provided.'

Even if the syllabus you are taking does not contain such a question, you would be wise to study this chapter carefully, because clarity and accuracy are important in all written English. This chapter also contains information on letter-writing, because the piece of factual writing you are asked to do is very often a letter. There is usually not much choice of question – sometimes no choice at all. Sometimes you are given all the material you need to complete your piece of writing; sometimes you have to make it up for yourself.

Here is a selection of the kinds of question that are set. They would not all, of course, be set in the same paper. Usually about half the time allowed for the essay is allowed for this question; and also about half the marks are awarded.

Factual writing

Answer one of the following. You should spend about 30 minutes on the question and write about one page.

1 *Explain, to a non-player, one of the following games: basketball, squash, whist, hockey.*
2 *Give instructions on how some waste material (for example bottle-tops, yoghurt cartons, cereal packets) can be used to make some toy or artwork. Give your piece of writing a heading.*

3 *You and some of your friends have had an idea on how to make good use of a piece of waste ground in your district (for example, to make a children's playground or a garden for old people). You and your friends are willing to do most of the hard work during your holidays. Write a letter to your local Youth Officer outlining your plan, and asking for his support in presenting it to the local council.*

4 *Your school or college has arranged an exhibition of arts and crafts. A leaflet giving details of each exhibit is to be provided for visitors. Write a general introduction to this leaflet.*

5 *You have learned that a pop festival is to be held in the near future in some open space near your home. Write a letter to your local newspaper either supporting or deploring the holding of this festival. Use some of the following points in your letter, and add some others of your own if you wish: noise going on all night – unmanageable crowds of young people – unsanitary conditions – hygiene well-arranged – young people must get together – litter – drugs – stealing from shops – money spent locally – cheap pleasure for thousands – have support of local police.*

6 *Answer both parts of this question.*

   (a) *Write, as secretary of one of the clubs or societies in your school or college, to some well-known personality in your field of interest, asking him or her to come to speak to your members next term.*

   (b) *Then, after your visitor has been to speak, write a short report (about ten to twelve lines) of the meeting for your local newspaper. Give the report a suitable headline.*

7 *Kate and Howard had grown up together as neighbours and school friends from early childhood – about a year ago, Kate moved away to another district when her father took a new job – they have not corresponded during this period, but they now realize they miss each other and would like to meet again – mother invites to come to stay.*

   Write a letter either from Kate to Howard, or from Howard to Kate, in which plans for this meeting are outlined.

Notice that half the pieces of writing you are asked to do in these questions consists of letters. This is about the usual proportion in any selections given for factual writing. (*NB* A letter also often appears in the selection for the essay question, so the information given here on the layout of letters will be useful for such a question, although for an answer to the essay question, the letter would, of course, be much longer than one page.) So, as such a high proportion of questions ask for a letter as an answer, we will deal with letters first of all. This is very useful information to know anyway.

Basically there are three different types of letter:

1 The business letter.
2 The formal letter.
3 The informal letter.

There is no exact division between these three types, but we will deal with them separately, so you can see the differences.

The business letter

It is unlikely that you will be asked to write a business letter in this examination, but so that you can recognize the different types, we will deal with it here.

A business letter is one written by one firm or organization to another, or to an individual, on business matters. It is nearly always written – or rather, typed – on headed paper which has printed on it the name, address, telephone (and sometimes telex) number, and often the name of the managing director etc., of the firm. A copy of the letter (made either by using carbon paper when it is being typed, or by using a photocopier) is always kept by the firm sending the letter. This is essential for future reference to see exactly what has been said in the correspondence.

Here is an example of a business letter:

SOUTHERN ELECTRONICS LIMITED

29 Poole Way, Southampton, SO6 7BT.

Telephone: 0703-61-485   *Telex*: 61-7147

Our Ref: SVC/ATL/CM   20 July, 1980.
Your Ref: NP/10/KT

The Managing Director,
Airspring Technics Ltd.,
Industrial Estate,
Warminster, Wilts.
WA2 6ZY

Dear Sir,
    Thank you for your inquiry dated 18 July about up-dating your computer system.
    As arranged by telephone today, Alan Roote, our Sales Manager, will be visiting you at

```
0930 hours on Monday, 31 July to have a
preliminary discussion about your
requirements.
                    Yours faithfully,
                    C. M. Cooley
                    (Managing Director)
```

Points to note about this letter

1 The first three lines, the name of the firm, the address and postal code, the telephone and telex numbers would be printed at the head of the writing paper. A well-designed heading for a firm's writing paper is most important, but there is no recognized layout. The tendency nowadays is to miss out all punctuation, to spread the heading right over the top of the page, and often to include some recognizable symbol.

2 All letters must be dated. The most usual position is on the right, as here. A form such as 20.vii.80 could be used, or 20.7.80, or 20.07.80, or 20 July '80; but that given is the best. Note the comma after July, and the full-stop after 1980. (The general point about punctuation in letters will be discussed fully later.)

3 The two references on the left-hand side. In their office, Southern Electronics Limited have a file tagged SVC/ATL. (The last two or three letters are usually the initials of the secretary who typed the letter.) The copy of this letter will go into this file with any future correspondence. Airspring Technics Limited have a file numbered NP/10, and the copy of their letter dated 18 July to Southern Electronics Limited will already be in this file. It will now be joined by the letter dated 20 July from Southern Electronics Limited. So all the correspondence between the two firms on this piece of business will be collected into separate files in the office of each company, and the reference number enables the secretaries to find the appropriate file immediately.

It is not usual for individuals to have reference numbers (even if they file their correspondence carefully). But an individual writing to a firm should always give the firm's reference number (if known), as 'Your Ref:' on the left at the head of the letter. This will enable the secretary of the firm to find the relevant correspondence quickly. Note the colon after 'Your Ref:', but no full-stop after Ref. although it is an abbreviation. (See p 144 in the chapter on punctuation.)

4 The person and address where the letter is being sent is given on the left-hand side before the letter itself begins. Alternatively, this can be given at the bottom of the letter after the signature, also on the left-hand side. In both cases, every line of the address starts directly in line with the margin. Note all the commas and the full-stop after the abbreviated name of the county, but no full-stop after the postcode.

5 The letter begins 'Dear Sir,' with a capital S for 'Sir,' followed by a comma.

6 The first word of the letter itself is indented from the left-hand margin.

7 The first word of each subsequent paragraph begins exactly under the first word of the first paragraph. This keeps the paragraphing clear.

8 The formal close to the letter is 'Yours faithfully,' with a small 'f' and a comma. 'Yours faithfully' is always used when the letter begins 'Dear Sir,' or 'Dear Madam,' i.e. without the person to whom the letter is sent being addressed by name. (Cf. Note 10 of the formal letter on p 37.)

9 There is no full-stop after the signature.

10 The position in the firm of the person signing the letter is often given, usually in brackets, after the signature.

NB The office practice for typing business letters has changed considerably over the last few years. There is a tendency to leave out all punctuation from addresses and dates, and to begin all paragraphs directly in line with the left-hand margin. It is possible, particularly when using a typewriter, to keep everything clear without all the punctuation marks – and the basic aim of punctuation, of course, is to make what you are writing clear to your reader. However, for the purposes of this English Language examination, you should include all the punctuation as given here, unless your examining board issues instructions to the contrary. The older conventions cannot be counted as wrong; the newer convention of leaving out all punctuation, might well be.

The formal letter

Formal letters are used when you are writing to a person in a formal, official capacity, rather than as a close friend. They include letters written to the press. Often, of course, a correspondence which begins by being formal, becomes more and more informal as the two people come to know each other better.

A formal letter is one you are most likely to be asked to write in this part of the examination. In fact, apart from 7, all the letters in the suggested questions on pp 31–2 are formal.

Here is an example of a formal letter which could be written in reply to 6 (a).

6(a)
```
                              Hamtown College,
                                High Street,
                                  Hamtown,
                                    Middlesex.
                                    HA6 ODP
                              21 July, 1980.
Dear Dr Waley,
   As secretary of the College Archaeological
Society, I have been asked to write to you to
see if you could come to speak to the members
of our society next term.  We usually meet at
4.15 on Thursday afternoons, but we would
be happy to arrange the meeting on any other
day or time that would suit you.  Any date in
October or November (apart from the last week
in October which is half-term holiday) would be
suitable for us.
   The subject of your talk we leave entirely to
you, although we should be very pleased to hear
something about your work at Paestum.
                         Yours sincerely,
                         Colin Carter
```

Points to note about this letter

1 The address of the college is written on the right-hand side of the sheet of paper, with an angle of about 45° between the lines, apart from the postcode which comes immediately under the name of the county.

2 There is a comma after each line of the address apart from the last, where there is a full-stop.

3 There is no full-stop after the postcode. The practice now seems to be established that postcodes are treated as a separate part of the address and are given with no punctuation.

4 The date is given immediately under the first line of the address.

The form given is the best. Note the comma after July, and the full-stop at the end of the date.

5 The address of the person to whom the letter is being written is, unlike the business letter, not given in a formal letter. Likewise, of course, there are no reference numbers.

6 The formal opening to the letter is 'Dear Dr Waley,' with a comma after the name. It is usual to use the title of the person addressed, such as Mr, or Dr, or Mrs, or Miss etc. (Cf. p 144 of the chapter on Punctuation to see why these abbreviations have no full-stop after them.)

7 The first word of the first paragraph is indented from the margin.

8 All subsequent paragraphs are also similarly indented from the margin.

9 The style of the letter is direct and clear; only essential information is given. The tone is straightforward and polite. When writing any kind of letter, try to visualize the person to whom the letter is being sent; you are then more likely to get the style and tone right.

10 The formal close is 'Yours sincerely,' with a small 's' and a comma.

11 The signature should be given clearly, without a full-stop. (If there is any doubt about the name, it can be given in block capitals in brackets underneath.)

The informal letter

This is a letter written between friends, two people who know each other well enough to be informal in their relationship with each other. It is, in fact, one of the stages in friendship when you can begin to be informal in your letters. Some people, when they come to know each other very well, write extremely informal letters, with private jokes and sometimes even a private language. But if you are asked to write an informal letter for this question in the examination, you would be unwise to make it too informal. Remember you are answering a question that is looking for clarity and accuracy.

Question 7 given earlier in this chapter could be an informal letter. Here is a possible answer:

Tel: Northwood 6721   26 Vincent Road,
                                          Northwood,
                                           Essex.
                                           HAO 4HH
                                        24 July, 1980.

Dear Kate,

   It seems ages since you moved away, but I
realize it is just about one year exactly.
Although I haven't written to you, I know that
I have been missing you a lot. We spent so
much time together when we were young that we
rather took each other's company for granted,
but now that you are no longer around, I
realize I am quite lonely at times.

   In fact, this is why I'm writing now. Would
you like to come down to spend a few days with
us during the holidays? Mum says she would be
very pleased to put you up, and it would be a
chance to see old places and old friends again.
Any time during August would be all right for
us. Perhaps you could give us a ring so we can
fix a time.

   Kind regards to your parents. I hope your
father likes his new job. But all the news
when we meet.

      Best wishes from all of us here,
                     Yours ever,
                     Howard

Points to note about this letter

1 The address is on the right-hand side, with a slope of 45° as in
   the formal letter, apart from the postcode.

2 There is a comma after the name of the road, and after the name
   of the town, and a full-stop after the name of the county. The
   postcode is left without punctuation.

3 The date comes immediately under the first line of the address,
   with a comma after the month and a full-stop after the year.
   The form used here is the best.

4 The telephone number is given on the left, with a colon after 'Tel:',
   but no full-stop at the end of the number. This is the most usual
   convention for giving a telephone number.

5 The letter begins close to the margin, with the conventional opening,
   'Dear Kate,' with a comma after the name of the person addressed.

6 The first word of the first paragraph is indented from the margin (which is imagined rather than actually drawn). All subsequent paragraphs also begin at the same distance from the margin.

7 The tone of the letter is friendly and informal, but not too much so. There is a tendency for some candidates, when asked to write an informal letter, to show off all their knowledge of the latest slang and swear-words; but remember this is an examination in your knowledge of the conventional rather than unconventional use of the English language.

8 All the points mentioned in the outline in the question come into the answer, but they are not over-elaborated. The letter is clear and straightforward.

9 It is usual to send 'Best wishes,' or some such friendly close, when writing to a friend. But notice that a comma comes after this greeting, even though the formal close (here 'Yours ever,') begins with a capital 'Y'.

10 The formal close, given on a separate line, begins with a capital letter and has a comma after it. The actual words used depend on the degree of friendship between the writer of the letter and the person addressed, but 'Yours ever,' or just 'Yours,' are good compromises between too much formality and too much intimacy.

11 The signature, without the surname, has no full-stop after it.

These three examples of letters do not exhaust all the possibilities of letter-writing; but they all demonstrate at least one thing – the careful attention you must pay to layout and detail. And as this part of the examination is designed to test your accuracy over detail, you can see why a letter is so often required as an answer to one of the questions. There is plenty of opportunity to lose marks through being careless over detail. If you want to gain a high mark for this question, you must learn all the conventions of letter-writing. These include the layout on the page; where to use capital letters and where not to use a capital letter; the appropriate opening and close; and, perhaps most important of all, the correct punctuation.

Punctuation has a chapter of its own in this book, but the punctuation of letters has some distinct rules of its own. (For example, a letter is one of the few pieces of writing which does not have a full-stop at the end, because there is no full-stop after the closing signature.) As was mentioned earlier, modern practice in some offices has developed a tendency to miss out all punctuation in addresses and dates, but the examiners of the English Language examination will expect you to know the more usual conventions, and you will be penalized if you don't get them right.

One part of learning correct punctuation is training your eyes to actually see all those little dots and commas. Some people have such difficulty with seeing the words correctly, that their eyes have no time for the punctuation. To train your eyes to actually see all the punctuation marks, go back to the three letters given in this chapter and count the punctuation marks used in each. (You can check your accuracy at the end of this chapter where the answers are given after the Examination practice on p 48.)

Letters to the press

Before leaving letter-writing, mention should be made of one further kind of letter that often appears in the questions, but of which an example has not yet been given: that is the letter to the press, be it to a newspaper or a magazine.

A letter to the press is of a rather special variety. Although it is addressed to the editor of the paper, the writer is not so much interested in only the editor reading it, but also all the thousands (or millions) of people who read that newspaper or magazine. Letters to the press can be very influential, both at a local and national (even international) level. Many decisions of local importance (such as building or not building a bypass or motorway) have been affected by correspondence in the local newspapers. Some important pieces of legislation at a national level (such as using children as photographic models for pornographic publications) have been instigated through letters to national newspapers. Letters to the press are, in fact, instruments of democracy.

So the writer of the letter really has to have two people in his mind's eye when he is writing to the press. First of all he has to visualize the editor, because if the editor does not like the letter, he will not publish it. The editor of a big national newspaper receives hundreds of letters every day, so he can be very selective in what he publishes. The letters he selects need not necessarily reflect the editorial policy of his paper, because a good editor likes controversy in his letter column; but they must be concise, accurate, well-expressed, and not abusive (because the editor must consider any possible legal action). Secondly, the writer of the letter must have his eye on the general reader whom he hopes is going to read his letter, and be influenced by it. If it is to affect the general reader favourably, it must be clear, accurate, and concise.

But it is the tone of a letter to the press that is particularly difficult to get right. You are probably writing because you want to influence the readers in some way. But you don't need to influence those who already think the same way as yourself; neither have you any hope of influencing the die-hards whose opinions are completely opposite to your own; it is the people who occupy the middle ground whom you hope to move in your direction. You will not do this with extreme views expressed in violent language. A well-balanced view, conceding something to the other side of the argument, expressed in calm and moderate language, is far more likely to win more opinions to your side.

There is a letter to the press amongst the selection of questions given on p 32 of this chapter, Question 5. Turn back and re-read this question.

This is just the kind of topic which always stirs up correspondence in the local press. The editor of the local newspaper will receive dozens of letters, many from the die-hards of both sides, and some of these he will probably publish, just to show how selfish and intolerant some people can be. Between these two extremes, however, there will be well-argued letters that are far more likely to sway public opinion. Here is how Question 5 could be answered. Remember that the question asks you to use some of the material provided, and add some of your own. The letter should be about one page long.

63 Bintry Place,
Clumphery,
Dorset.
DT6 4LA
2nd June, 1980.

Sir,
    Having read in your columns of the intention
to hold a pop festival on the Common on
Midsummer Eve, I should like to support the
proposal. I am not a young person myself, but
I can appreciate the need for today's young
people to come together to enjoy their own
festival with the kind of music they like.
    I expect the usual arguments will be put
forward about drugs and litter and stealing; no
doubt some abuses will take place, but no more
than usual when large numbers of people come
together. There are always a few rogues in
every crowd. However, I understand that the
organizers have been in touch with the local

police, and have their approval for the general
arrangements for crowd control and sanitation.
There is also an agreement to clear up all the
litter.

I expect there will also be the usual
arguments about noise going on well into the
night, keeping old people and children awake.
But these arguments are never put forward when
the annual Michaelmas Fair is held on the
Common.   That, of course, is seen as part of
the local folklore, and so can be justified.   I
imagine these young people are attempting to
revive an even older tradition by holding their
festivities on the Common on Midsummer Eve.   I
wish I were young enough to join them.

>Yours, etc.,
>Joseph Fenton

Points to note about this letter

1 The address is written on the right, with the usual punctuation.
2 The date is given immediately under the address. The form, 2nd
   June, 1980. (instead of 2 June, 1980.) now looks rather old-fashioned,
   but it can be used. But note the punctuation. (Why is there no full-
   stop after 2nd, although it is an abbreviation?)
3 The letter begins 'Sir,' (note the comma) and not 'Dear Sir'. 'Dear
   Sir,' could be used, but there is a convention to use just 'Sir,' when
   writing to the press.
4 The first word of the first paragraph is indented from the margin,
   as are all the subsequent paragraphs.
5 The tone of the letter is mild and calm. It is clear and concise, recog-
   nizes the other point of view, but makes no doubt about which side
   the writer supports. It might antagonize some of the die-hards;
   but it is quite likely to make some people think again.
6 The letter ends 'Yours, etc.,' (note the full-stop and commas).
   This again is a conventional ending to a letter to the press, but 'Yours
   faithfully,' could be used instead.
7 There is no full-stop after the signature.
8 The letter is correct in every detail of layout and punctuation. It is in
   clear and accurate English. It makes use of the material provided
   in the question, adding just one or two extra ideas. It fulfils the
   instruction from one of the question papers given earlier in this
   chapter: 'You should understand that this question is designed to

test your accuracy in the writing of English and in your use of the material provided.' It would be all too easy, in a question such as this, where you could become emotionally swayed, to become involved in your argument rather than in your accuracy. But the English Language examination is concerned with accuracy, not with argument. Many candidates forget this basic point, become emotionally involved, and so make many careless errors.

Instructions and reports

Letters are not the only kind of writing required in this part of the examination. Turn back to pp 31–2 and read the questions again: 1, 2, 4 and 6 (b) are typical of another type of required writing: i.e. factual instructions or reports.

Nothing has been said, as yet, about making a plan for this question. Generally, because the question is so short, most people can make and hold a plan in their head. The plan is not so elaborate as that needed for an essay, and is often suggested by the material given in the question itself.

However, if you feel that a plan helps you to keep your ideas clear in even a short piece of writing, you can easily make a very brief plan in just a few seconds. The last letter given in this chapter, for example, could have been planned thus:

Paragraph 1: not young, but support.

Paragraph 2: some abuse inevitable – arrangements approved by police.

Paragraph 3: no objection to traditional Michaelmas Fair – Midsummer Eve older tradition.

This is enough to hold the outline in front of you.

In a question which asks you to give instructions, it is perhaps better to make a very brief plan. Otherwise your instructions, which should be clear, could easily become jumbled up. Question 2 is a good example of such a question:

2 Give instructions on how some waste material (for example, bottle-tops, yoghurt cartons, cereal packets) can be used to make some toy or artwork. Give your piece of writing a heading.

You need to pause and think for a moment about how your instructions are going to be arranged, and then jot down one or two words. The instructions should follow the sequence of actions that must be taken. For example, imagine we are going to give instructions on how to make a painted design out of old bottle-tops. The sequence of events will be:

1 Collecting materials (bottle-tops, adhesive, hardboard, spray paint)
2 Sorting
3 Outline design
4 Sticking
5 Spraying
6 Framing

A little bit of thought while making this outline will ensure that you miss nothing out, so your finished piece of writing is clear and tidy. If you rush straight into your piece of writing, you can all too easily find you have missed out one vital stage, which then means time-consuming rewriting, or untidy alterations.

Here is how Question 2 could be completed, using the outline given above.

DESIGNS FROM BOTTLE-TOPS

Interesting designs can be made from old bottle-tops. You must, first of all, collect a large quantity of bottle-tops of different sizes. You also need a piece of hardboard cut to a suitable shape and size; some good adhesive to stick the bottle-tops on to the hardboard; some paint – the aerosol spray type is best; and, if possible, a frame to fit the hardboard.

Sort the bottle-tops into similar sizes and types; they are much more effective when grouped rather than used indiscriminately. Then outline your design on the hardboard with pencil or crayon, and select which tops are going to be used for each part. The biggest tops give the boldest outlines; small tops are good for background patterns. A really big top from a jar can make a good central feature of a design.

You are now ready to begin sticking the bottle-tops on to the hardboard. Cover small areas of the hardboard with adhesive (not too much, or it will dry out), and press on the tops, making sure they are exactly in place and firmly stuck. (They can be used either way up, but the top, of course, gives a much bigger area for adhesion.) Continue applying the adhesive and the bottle-tops until the whole design has been completed.

The most effective way to paint the design is to use an aerosol spray. One colour, such as gold or silver, will bring out the force of a good design. When framed, such a design makes a most effective wall decoration.

Points to note about these instructions

1 They have been given a heading, which the question asked for. It is easy to forget a small detail such as this, and so miss the two or three marks allowed for a good heading.

2 They are written in continuous prose and not as notes. For several of the questions set in this part of the examination, you might be tempted to use numbered notes, tables, diagrams, plans or maps: instructions and factual information are very often most effectively conveyed with the use of such devices. But remember this is an examination in your use of language (words and punctuation); so, unless you are given specific instructions to the contrary, you should not use such devices. The question is designed to test your accurate and effective use of language.

3 Notice how the paragraphing helps to clarify the different stages of the process. You can tell you have come to a new stage of what you have to do because you have come to a new paragraph. (The outline plan has six stages. If you were writing these instructions for a children's magazine, it would probably be better to simplify them by numbering them from 1 to 6, as in the outline plan. But as a piece of continuous writing, they fit effectively into four paragraphs. However six paragraphs would not be out-of-place, although two – sorting and framing – would be very short.)

4 The instructions are clear and easy to follow. They are kept as brief as possible, and no superfluous information is given, just enough to suggest how the most effective use can be made of the materials. Instructions can easily become confusing if they are cluttered with too much detail.

5 Look carefully at the punctuation. Notice how many semi-colons there are. The semi-colon is a most effective punctuation mark for helping to sort out complex activities or ideas. There is also an effective use made of a dash – and of brackets (which are more likely to be used in notes or instructions than in a composition). But to gain a high mark in this question, every punctuation mark must be clear and accurate. These simple instructions demonstrate the necessity for a complete understanding of punctuation. Your command of the English language then becomes so much more effective.

6 Look carefully at the vocabulary used. Such words as 'adhesive', 'aerosol', 'indiscriminately', 'feature', 'adhesion', 'effective', help to keep the instructions concise and clear. But you must be confident

that you can spell such words, because misspelt words will lose marks in this question.

7 So long as they make sense, it doesn't matter if the instructions you give are entirely accurate *as instructions*. For example, it might be better here to apply the adhesive to the actual bottle-tops rather than to the hardboard. You are not being tested on the effectiveness of the instructions (as you would be in an examination in Design Technology), but in the accuracy of your English.

Before leaving this part of the examination, let us look at one further question, or rather part of a question which has so far not been completed.

6 *Answer both parts of this question.*
   (*a*) *Write, as secretary of one of the clubs or societies in your school or college, to some well-known personality in your field of interest, asking him or her to come to speak to your members next term.*
   (*b*) *Then, after your visitor has been to speak, write a short report (about ten to twelve lines) of the meeting for your local newspaper. Give the report a suitable headline.*

The first part of this question has already been completed as the formal letter on p 36.

Here is how the second part of the question could be completed:

6(*b*)   EXCAVATIONS AT PAESTUM

Dr Sara Waley, the well-known archaeologist, spoke last Thursday afternoon at Hamtown College to members of the College Archaeological Society. Dr Waley has spent several seasons recently on the excavations at Paestum, not far from Salerno in Italy.

Paestum was originally a Greek outpost, but it developed a distinct culture of its own, particularly characteristic being the painted tombs. Dr Waley showed many slides, including some of the famous 'diver', where a young man, after death, plunges into the waves of another life.

The talk was enjoyed by a large number of staff and students.

Points to note on this report
1 It is given a heading, as was asked for in the question. Always make sure you do everything the question asks you to do. The examiners allot a certain proportion of the marks to each part of the question, and if you miss out one part, you automatically miss the marks for that part.

2 Including the title, it takes up about 10–12 lines of writing, which is
  the number of lines allowed. This means the report must be very
  brief and can include only the main points, which must include the
  name of the speaker, the place and the subject.

3 If you were attempting a question such as this yourself, you would,
  of course, choose a speaker (real or made-up) who could talk on a
  subject on which you could write a short report because you have
  some first-hand interest and information on it.

4 The report is numbered 6 (b), as the letter was numbered 6 (a).
  Although, here, the division of the parts of the question is obvious,
  get into the habit of always numbering your answers in exactly the
  same way as the questions are numbered. It is not always obvious to
  the examiner which question, or part of a question, a candidate is
  supposed to be answering, and he is not going to waste time
  trying to sort out what you could so easily have made clear.

This part of the examination, where it does appear in the syllabus of
an examining board, often tends to be neglected. Plenty of time is spent
writing essays and summaries, but it is often assumed that factual
writing will look after itself.

However, it is not easy to write good letters which hit just the right
tone and are accurate in every detail. It needs constant practice to acquire the skill, and to make a habit of laying out all the parts of a letter
correctly and accurately.

Neither is it easy to write good, simple, clear, accurate instructions
or reports. This again is an acquired skill which comes only after constant practice.

And when you have completed writing your answer for this part of
the examination, it goes without saying that you must check it over very
carefully to make sure every detail is correct, every comma in place and
clear. This question is usually marked on a negative basis: that is, you
begin with a maximum possible mark, then have one mark deducted
for every mistake you make. So you cannot afford to leave it peppered
with small errors. And here again, correcting your own work is a skill
that can only be learned with practice. Make a habit of doing it for all
your written work, not just for your English work.

Use some of the questions given earlier in this chapter for practice,
including some that have already been answered, but using your own
material with the answers given here as a model. Then attempt some
more questions from the following exercises.

Examination practice

(Each answer to be about one page long, and to be completed in 30 minutes.)

1 *A friend is going to spend a holiday at a place you know well. Write a letter to this friend, suggesting places of interest that should be visited, special things to do etc.*

2 *Write a letter to the manager of your local swimming pool or sports centre asking if there is any possibility of a holiday job. Give your qualifications and interests.*

3 *You are in charge of some younger pupils who are going on a camping weekend. Write a letter to their parents outlining the arrangements, meeting place and return time, the equipment to be taken etc.*

4 *You have been asked by your local Youth Officer to suggest ways in which local amenities could be improved for young people. Write a report outlining your suggestions. Give the report a heading.*

5 *You have been asked by your local newspaper to send in a report of some outstanding event at your school or college (it could be sporting, cultural, a visit of some important person etc.) Write this report. Give it a suitable headline.*

6 *Select a place about a mile from where you live. Then, without using maps or diagrams, give a stranger who does not know the district, instructions on how to reach that place from your home.*

(Answers to number of punctuation marks in the letters: business letter: 35; formal letter: 20; informal letter: 29.)

3 Summary

After the essay, for most examining boards the summary is the most important single question. With some boards the summary is given as a separate question with a separate passage; but on most examination papers it is combined with the comprehension questions. Even if the questions do not begin with words such as '*Summarize in your own words ...*', you can recognize the questions which are intended for summary because they have more marks allotted to them, and the instructions usually give the number of words allowed for the answer.

Apart from the purposes of this examination, the ability to write a good summary is a most useful skill to acquire. It can help you with all your other studies, and also in many situations in real life. People are always saying, 'Tell me, briefly, what it's all about.' And that, really, is asking for a summary.

The ability to write a good summary is central to the use of English because it requires two essential elements of language: comprehension and composition – the ability to understand what somebody else has written, and then to put that person's information or ideas into your own words. It calls, as we shall see, for many different language skills: for the ability to concentrate on the passage and read with real understanding, seeing the implications behind the words as well as the surface meaning; for the ability to transpose this meaning into your own words, which calls for flexibility of sentence construction; for good punctuation; and, most important, for a good vocabulary, because you are then more likely to be able to find the one word or phrase which will sum up a concept that has taken twenty or thirty words to express in the original passage. In fact, to summarize, the writing of summary needs comprehension in depth, flexibility of sentence construction, good punctuation and a wide vocabulary.

A few boards ask the candidates to write a summary of a whole passage in a given number of words. Most boards, however, ask for what could be called selective summary; you are not asked to write a summary of the whole passage, but on one or two particular topics that are dealt with in the passage, so you have to read selectively and pick out what the author has to say in the passage on these topics. Both kinds of summary will be explained in this chapter.

But we will begin with a précis (which is another word for summary) of a whole passage, because that is a good place to begin to learn some of the basic skills of summary writing. Here is a typical question. Note the words to the instructions carefully.

Using not more than 100 words, write a summary of the following passage. Write in clear, concise English and use your own words as far as possible, although you may retain words or brief expressions which cannot be accurately or economically replaced. At the end you must state the exact number of words you have used. The original passage contains 329 words.

I have heard it said that the Olympic Games are the only festival of antiquity which a modern crowd would have understood. And this may be true. Apart from the sacrifice of boars at the beginning of the festival and the sacrifice of oxen at the end of it, there was nothing about the Olympic Games which a spectator from Huddersfield would not have appreciated as readily as a spectator from Ithaca or Thessaly. The modern visitor to Olympia would have seen nothing remarkable in the foot races and the various jumping contests. Television in its more lavish moments would no doubt have prepared him for the excitement of the chariot races in the Hippodrome. He would even recognize in the terrible physical ordeal of the Pancratium – a sight that probably would have horrified our bull-baiting ancestors of the last century – nothing more remarkable than our all-in wrestling. He would not have been surprised by the partisanship and by the tremendous local enthusiasm, for is not the same thing happening at every football match today? But surely he would have been astonished by the strange mixture of religion and athletics, the queer blend of a pilgrimage atmosphere with that of the Derby, which must have characterized the great festival in the Valley of Alpheus.

Every four years heralds proclaimed a sacred peace throughout the Greek world. Warring states laid down their arms and turned their attention to the Olympic Games. The Spartans loved to excel in all those contests which demanded endurance and stamina. The Ionians, on the other hand, shone in the more graceful sports. Boeotia provided the most famous wrestlers, Aegina the toughest boxers, and so on. Along all the roads that lead to Olympia great crowds pressed in the dust and heat of summer: runners, wrestlers, boxers, horsemen, charioteers, and also thousands of spectators anxious to watch their team, or champion, win the crown of wild olive. (329 words)

From *Middle East*, by H. V. Morton (Methuen).

There are four stages to writing a summary:
1 Understanding.
2 Detailed study.
3 Rough draft.
4 Finished copy.

1 **Understanding** It is obvious enough that you cannot write a good summary of a passage if you don't understand what it is about. So the first thing you have to do is to understand what the passage is saying.

Don't be alarmed if, after your first reading, you have no notion of what the passage is driving at. It is quite usual, particularly under the strained conditions of the examination, for the first reading not to make sense. You can be assured that the passage does make sense, and this will be revealed by your second or third readings, which should be slower and calmer than the first.

There are often one or two difficult or new words in the passage that can put you off at the first reading because they assume undue importance. Some of the names in this passage – Ithaca, Thessaly, Alpheus, Spartans, Ionians, Boeotia, Aegina – could put you off if you know little about Ancient Greece. It's most likely that you don't know what the Pancratium was either.

On your second reading you will, however, realize that the strange names are just different parts of Greece, and it doesn't matter that you don't know exactly where they are. And neither does it matter that you don't know exactly what the Pancratium was; it was obviously some sort of terrible physical ordeal rather like all-in wrestling. The passage explains it for you.

When you feel that you do understand the passage, for your own convenience summarize, in your head and not on paper, the general drift in one sentence. (This will not form part of your finished summary, but it is like the summary of the main events given at the beginning of a television news bulletin. The news items themselves are summaries of the thousands of words which pour into the television news offices every day.)

The sentence which you should have made up for yourself to grasp the general argument of the passage should have been something like: Of all the ancient festivals, the Olympic Games would have been, possibly, the only one understood by modern man, although he would have found the religious atmosphere perplexing.

2 **Detailed study** When you have, probably at your second reading, grasped the general sense of the passage, you are ready to re-read the passage, slowly and carefully, and make a list of the various points that the author had to make on his subject. Often these various points can themselves be subdivided. There are really four main points that the author makes about the Olympic Games, and two of them have sub-divisions:

1 Olympic Games only ancient festival understood by modern man.
   (This argument is not necessarily the opinion of the writer: he says: 'I have heard it said', and adds: 'This may be true.' The finished summary should make this clear.)
2 Similarities between then and now:
   (a) Track and field events, even Pancratium;
   (b) Rivalry of supporters;
   (c) Chariot races on television. (It is debatable whether the chariot races should be included or not. What is important here is that the author is allowing the modern man's lack of surprise to be based on his having seen television, and this important point is not introduced elsewhere into the argument. It should, therefore, be included.)
3 The religious atmosphere, sacrifices, perplexing. (The sacrifices, although mentioned earlier in the original, are making the same point as 'he would have been astonished by the strange mixture of religion and athletics', and so are not included separately as we cannot waste words by repeating.)
4 The original Games:
   (a) Peace every four years;
   (b) Specialization by different States;
   (c) Competitors and spectators made for Olympia.

Each point should be numbered and set out systematically on a piece of rough paper. It is important to keep this so-called 'rough work' clear and orderly, because then the writing of your summary is more likely to be clear and orderly. It is all too easy for a summary to dissolve into a vague muzziness, rather like an out-of-focus photograph. In a good summary, every point should be clear and sharply in focus.

When you have finished your slow and careful re-reading, and the making of your notes, you should have, in note form, the substance of the passage. If you have made your notes efficiently, you should be able to write your summary without consulting the original passage again. However, it is safer to re-read the passage yet again to make sure that nothing of importance has been omitted. The descriptive detail of 'the dust and heat of summer' tells us at what time of the year the Games were held: this is important, so it must be included, not as description, but as fact. This one important point about the time of the year would probably be allotted one mark by the examiners, and to miss it out would forfeit that one mark.

3 Rough draft You are now ready to write, in rough, your first draft of your summary. Remember what the instructions to the question said: '*Write in clear, concise English and use your own words as far as possible, although you may retain words or brief expressions which cannot be accurately or economically replaced.*'

When you have finished your rough copy, count the number of words you have used. Most examining boards give you a number which must not be exceeded. If you have used more than you are allowed, do not just cross out one sentence, because this probably contains one important point, but find some way to express the ideas in less words.

If you are more than ten words under the number allowed, you have probably missed out something that should have been included. Find out what it is by reading through the passage again.

It is very rare for the first draft of a summary to arrive at the correct number of words. Several additions or deletions are usually needed. This means alterations and corrections. This is why it is essential to write a rough copy. You should hand in a summary that is neat and easy to read. Examiners like to see neatly corrected work, but they do not like to waste time trying to find their way through work which is full of untidy alterations and insertions.

The original version of the summary given below contained 107 words, and many alterations were made before it arrived at its present form. If you write your first draft in rough, you can then alter and rearrange as much as you like, and still hand in a finished copy which is neat and easy to mark.

4 Finished copy When your summary has arrived at the correct number of words (not more than ten under the amount allowed), you are ready to write out, neatly and legibly, the finished copy you are going to hand in. When you have written it out, read it through carefully. It is very easy to make mistakes, such as missing out a word, when copying. The finished copy is given below:

The conjecture that the Olympic Games would have been the only ancient festival understood by modern man, is possibly sound. The track and field events, even the Pancratium, have their modern counterparts, as have the rivalries of enthusiastic supporters. Television has shown chariot races. However, the religious atmosphere pervading the original Games, which opened and closed with sacrifices, would have perplexed a modern audience. Every fourth summer all wars stopped in the Greek world, and the States, each specializing in its chosen sport, concentrated on the Games. The competitors, with their thousands of supporters, made for Olympia.

There is one more thing you must do. What is it? Remember the instructions to the question: '*At the end you must state the exact number of words you have used.*' Don't attempt to cheat here by writing down fewer words than you have actually used. (It often happens in examinations.) An examiner, after marking forty or fifty summaries, can judge the number of words just about exactly. Using too many words is penalized; but dishonesty is penalized even more. The summary above contains 97 words.

There are three other points that should be made here:
1 Timing.
2 Using your own words.
3 Ways to save words.

Timing It will probably appear that you have so much to do – reading the passage three or four times; making notes; then making a rough copy; then writing out a finished copy – that there is not enough time to complete all this in the examination. It certainly does need real concentration, an efficient technique, and no time-wasting.

The time allowed in the examination for the summary varies, and is usually at the candidate's discretion, because the summary question is one of several on a paper, and not a paper on its own. However, you should remember that the summary usually carries quite a high percentage of marks, and so it is worth allotting a proportionate amount of time to this question. It usually works out to something between 30 and 45 minutes.

It does not take long to read a passage of 350 or 500 words, even slowly and carefully. (Time yourself over this.) It does not take long to write out a rough copy of about 100 or 120 words, and then a finished copy of the same length. (Time yourself with this too.) It is the second part of summary writing – the more detailed study and making of notes – that takes the most time. But that is how it should be, because that is really the heart of the matter. It is the efficiency with which you complete the second part that really decides how good your summary is going to be.

So you need to ascertain, from the time given for the paper on which your summary question appears, how long you can spend on this question. If the summary question (or questions – there are sometimes more than one) is taken from the same passage as that set for the comprehension questions, you then obviously save on some of the reading time.

When you do know how many minutes you can allow yourself for this question, you then need to practise writing summaries of the length required by your board. Use a passage of about the same length as is set by your board, time carefully your reading, your more detailed study and note-making, rough copy, and finished copy. With practice, you will find they can all be fitted into the time allowed.

Using your own words   The instructions to nearly all summary questions advise you to *use your own words*. Some instructions also add: *You may use words and short expressions from the passage, but large-scale copying will be penalized.*

This seemingly contradictory advice often causes confusion. What does it mean exactly? There are some good examples in the summary we have already looked at in this chapter, and we will have further examples later. What the examiners want to see is that you have absorbed the information and ideas in the passage so you can express them in your own words as if it were you giving this information and ideas and not the original author.

But, of course, if the passage is about the Olympic Games, you must use the same phrase in your summary. The words 'festival', 'sacrifice', 'religion', 'atmosphere', 'sport', 'Pancratium', 'chariot races', 'summer', appear in both the original passage and the finished summary. It would be difficult to write about the Olympic Games, saying what

H. V. Morton said about them, without using these words. But you feel they have been absorbed into the thinking of the writer of the summary, and are not just copied from the original passage.

But look at what happens to some of the other words and phrases: 'festival of antiquity' becomes 'ancient festival'; 'spectator' becomes 'supporter'; 'foot races and the various jumping contests' becomes 'track and field events'; 'heralds proclaimed a sacred peace' becomes 'all wars stopped'. There are many more examples. The writer of the summary is using his own words. H. V. Morton has a rather florid style; the writer of the summary uses a very plain, straightforward style. That is what you should aim at when you *use your own words*. Don't use any words from the passage other than those that are essential for thinking about the contents of the passage. All the other words, and the style of writing, should be your own.

Ways of saving words It goes without saying that when you are writing a summary with a limit to the number of words, you should not waste any words. You need to express the information and ideas in the briefest number of words. But, at the same time, you have to write your summary 'in good continuous prose'. This means you cannot use a note form which misses out small words such as *the, a, some* etc. (unless the question specifically asks for this).

How then can you save words? We have already seen some examples in the previous section on 'Using your own words'. Did you notice how 'festival of antiquity' (3 words) became 'ancient festival' (2 words); 'foot races and the various jumping contests' (7 words) became 'track and field events' (4 words); and 'heralds proclaimed a sacred peace' (5 words) became 'all wars stopped' (3 words)? All these examples of *using your own words* also *save words*. When attempting to express the information and ideas of the original passage in your own words, you must try to find words and phrases that will express them in less words. There is no sense in using your own words for any point in the original if it means you are going to use more words than the original. Remember the instructions said: '*You may retain words or brief expressions which cannot be accurately or economically replaced.*' All the words that appeared in both the original and summary were of this kind; but all the examples of using your own words also saved words. This is how it should be.

But there are also, in this summary, many more examples of saving words. Remember the first point made in the notes on the 'Detailed study' of this passage: that the argument was not necessarily that of the writer, because he says: 'I have heard it said', and adds: 'This may be true.' This is quite a difficult point to make in few words, but the two words 'the conjecture' make it quite clear that the view being expressed is not necessarily that of the author. This one word 'conjecture' saves many words.

There are other examples. All the different Greek States that are named in the original passage are reduced to 'the States'; there is no space to name all of them, so none is mentioned: all are reduced to one collective noun. The same happens to 'runners', 'wrestlers', 'boxers', 'horsemen', 'charioteers'; they become 'competitors'. And notice, too, what happens to the long list of sports that the various States excelled in: 'The Spartans loved to excel . . . Aegina the toughest boxers, and so on' (39 words) becomes 'the States, each specializing in its chosen sport' (8 words).

Another way to save words is to make sure that nothing is repeated in your summary, even if it is repeated in the original passage. The 'sacrifices' and 'religious atmosphere' are mentioned in two separate places in the original passage; but they are brought together into one sentence in the summary. To repeat points is to waste words; and this is penalized.

We will turn now to the second type of summary, what was called earlier a *selective summary*, that is not a summary of the whole passage, but of some of the information or ideas expressed in the passage. This kind of summary is used by most boards; some set a separate passage for this selective passage; others include the selective summary (or summaries) among their comprehension questions, and so set them on the same passage. But in either case, the techniques involved are the same, except, of course, in the latter case, you don't have to read separate passages for both comprehension and summary, so you save some time on reading.

Apart from the fact that not all the information or ideas in the passage must be summarized, but only those relevant to the questions set, the principles are the same as those for a précis of the whole passage:

1 Understanding the original passage.
2 More detailed study, but here picking out those parts that are relevant to the questions set.
3 Writing a rough draft.
4 Making a finished copy of your answer.

And the three other points also apply:

1 Time yourself carefully.
2 Use your own words as far as possible.
3 Find ways to save words.

The set passage need not be a piece of straightforward prose; it could be part of a play or a recorded discussion, as is the following passage:

In one paragraph of not more than 100 words, summarize what the speakers in the following discussion have to say about the education of young people of today for citizenship in the 21st Century. Use your own words as far as possible.

Chairman   This must be one of the most difficult times to attempt to plan education for the future, when you realize that the young people in our schools and colleges will be the mature citizens of the next century. What are some of the problems?

Mr A   Well I suppose one of the most difficult is that nothing is stable any longer. There have been so many new developments over the last few years, and they are likely to continue at an ever-increasing rate.

Chairman   What kind of new developments?

Mr A   There has really been a new industrial revolution, and I don't think we have yet felt the main impact. The new generation of computers will have shattering effects.

Chairman   What do you think, Mrs B?

Mrs B   I think I tend to agree. One of the main impacts will be on employment. So many jobs in factories and warehouses will disappear. There is a lot of talk about modernizing industry, but what that really means is that the whole process will be controlled by a computer with one or two specialized engineers. The same thing is going to happen in offices too. A telephone call – or more probably a television call – will automatically be recorded and filed, so there will be no need for so many secretaries and typists.

Chairman   You'll still need someone to make the boss's tea!

Mrs B   That often comes out of a machine already!

Chairman   What you're saying is that we really have to educate young people to face unemployment.

Mr A   Well the prospect does look as if there will inevitably be more unemployment because there will not be so many jobs.

Mrs B   Unless, of course, we organize things differently, and everybody works much shorter hours.

Mr A And then everybody has more time of their own to spend, so they have to be educated in how to make sensible use of the hours when they are not working.

Chairman You don't think everyone will be whizzing off to the moon, or space, in the 21st Century?

Mrs B Who knows? But I think myself all this space business is a lot of . . . well . . . not exactly nonsense . . . but I feel Man is a creature of this planet.

Mr A I'm not so sure. One feature of Man's development so far has been his adventurous spirit.

Mrs B But unless we conquer Time, there's nowhere worth getting to within our solar system in the time we could get there.

Mr A Unless, of course, we put up vast satellites for people to live in.

Mrs B But I can't imagine people living in such claustrophobic conditions.

Mr A When cavemen moved out into the plains, they probably couldn't stand the wide open spaces to begin with.

Chairman But I think we ought to get back to the education of young people.

Mrs B I don't think it is entirely irrelevant. What it does indicate is that the change will continue at such a rate that one of the few things we can be sure about is that if they are going to survive, the young people of today are going to have to accept change, and to be willing to change themselves and to fit into all sorts of conditions which are unforeseeable now.

Mr A And there is another aspect we have not touched on. This planet has only limited supplies of oil, coal, iron, even water – all the things needed for development. Young people must be taught the full meaning of being citizens of the world, what the implications are, otherwise everybody is going to be fighting for the diminishing supplies of the essentials.

Mrs B And we now, of course, not only with the Bomb, but with chemical and bacteriological warfare, have the power to wipe out mankind altogether.

Chairman Not a happy future.

Mr A Who knows? The thing is, it's really impossible to foretell the future. Something that no one has thought of might suddenly turn up, which would make all our proposals seem like a lot of nonsense.

Chairman Let's hope it's something pleasant.

Most of this passage is about the education of young people; the section in the middle about space travel is only incidentally relevant. It doesn't matter how much you were interested in the points raised by the speakers about space travel, you must not include them in your answer. What you have to do is to summarize in one paragraph of not more than 100 words what the speakers have to say about *the education of young people of today for citizenship in the 21st Century*.

This passage is much longer than the previous one studied in this chapter, although the number of words allowed for the summary is the same; but not all the passage has to be summarized. However, even those parts of the discussion that are relevant to the question contain more words than the whole passage about the Olympic Games. This means that the summary will have to be more concentrated. More words will have to be saved.

One technique of summary writing that we have noted already is that *using your own words* and *saving words* should amount to the same thing. Part of the process of the more detailed study of the passage should be the purposeful attempt to find groups of words which can be expressed in one collective word or phrase, thus saving many words. There are many examples in this passage. Read through the discussion again, looking for concepts that can be expressed in one or two words. For example, Mr A talks about everybody having 'more time of their own to spend', and the 'hours when they are not working'. This can be summed up in one word which is not used in the discussion: 'leisure'. Try to find other examples before reading on. This is where a good vocabulary is so useful.

That part of the discussion which is about 'so many new developments over the last few years', and 'the new industrial revolution' could be summed up in one phrase such as 'rapid technological developments'.

The point that Mrs B makes about these developments is that 'the whole process will be controlled by a computer' and that 'many jobs . . . will disappear', because (she implies) they will be done automatically by machines and not by people. All this could be summarized in the one phrase 'computerized automation'.

Then Mrs B goes further. She suggests this process will take place not only in industry, but also 'in offices . . . so there will be no need for so many secretaries and typists'. These two could be brought together in a phrase such as 'industrial and commercial enterprises'.

What about Mrs B's point that 'young people of today are going to have to accept change, and to be willing to change themselves and to fit into all sorts of conditions which are unforeseeable now'? This could all be summed up in two words: 'adaptability' and 'flexibility'.

'Supplies of oil, coal, iron, even water – all the things needed for development' can be reduced to the one word 'resources'.

'Everybody is going to be fighting' becomes the one word 'competition'.

So after our more detailed study we could have notes such as the following:

1 Difficult to educate for 21st Century.
2 Rapid technological development – computerized automation in industrial and commercial enterprises – more unemployment – more leisure.
3 Education for
   (a) adaptability, flexibility and use of leisure
   (b) world citizenship or competition for limited resources will lead to war and destruction of Man.
4 Unforeseen developments = all plans wrong.

These notes could then, after writing a rough copy which could be altered and adapted, lead to a summary such as the following:

It is difficult to assess how best to educate young people today for citizenship in the 21st Century. Rapid technological developments, particularly in computerized automation, will eliminate many employment opportunities in industrial and commercial enterprises. There will probably be more unemployment, or shorter working hours. Rapid changes will continue, so education for adaptability, flexibility, and the use of leisure is desirable. The responsibilities of world citizenship must also be taught, otherwise competition for the limited resources of the planet could lead to war, even the destruction of mankind. But unforeseen developments could cause all these plans to be completely wrong. (99 words)

This is 99 words, so it is the right length. It is quite good, but it could be improved. There is one small point that Mrs B makes that has been missed out; that is that jobs will be lost in 'warehouses' as well as in 'factories' and 'offices'. 'Warehouses' could, perhaps, be included in the phrase 'industrial enterprises'. But then we realize we could save two words in this sentence: 'will eliminate employment opportunities in industrial and commercial enterprises' could become, more simply, 'will eliminate many jobs in factories and offices' (8 words). So we can now include 'warehouses' and change the phrase to 'will eliminate many jobs in factories, warehouses and offices' (9 words).

This is the kind of small improvement and correction that can be made at the rough-copy stage. And notice we have abandoned our original phrases 'employment opportunities' and 'industrial and commercial enterprises' for the more simple words 'jobs' and 'factories and offices' because they are accurate, and they save words.

This is the kind of flexible attitude you must have when writing a summary. Never allow your various versions to be too fixed, until, of course, you come to the finished copy you are going to hand in. Even then, given time, you could probably make some further small improvement. Summary writing is not something automatic. It is an activity requiring flexibility, adaptability and decision making. And, because your time is limited, you must finally decide on the finished version you are going to hand in.

Sometimes the summary question calls for the writing of two paragraphs on two different topics discussed in the passage, or two separate questions altogether. If this is so, each part of the summary is often shorter, about 60 or 70 words being allowed for each part. Here are two such questions which would be included with the comprehension questions (not given here), so the passage is a longer one.

Read the following passage carefully, and then answer the questions underneath. Use your own words as far as possible, keep within the given number of words for each answer, and, in answering, use only information that is contained in the passage.

This is a true story with a triple theme. It tells firstly of a brook or stream, 'common' in the sense that it is but one of a thousand such streams which spring from the folds of hills everywhere, and especially in the chalklands of East Anglia. This particular stream rises a few miles to the south-east of Royston and meanders gently on a mere ten-mile course to join the River Rhee. In order to find it today you would need a large-scale map, and you would need to know exactly where to look for it, because the stream has no name, nor ever had, other than 'Brook'. Even the local inhabitants are for the most part unaware of its existence. And having found it, you also would have some doubts; for in places the stream has been filled in and it flows, if at all, in an underground pipe. In other places it is so overgrown with nettles and reeds and tall grasses that you might well fall into it before you knew that it was there. In yet other places, especially in a dry season, you could walk dryfoot along its bed for long stretches, as do the hares and pheasants. Only the willows mark its course with any real prominence, and even they, stricken by age and neglect, are fast disappearing; for no one, it seems, ever thinks of replanting a willow. How can such a miserable stream, such a symbol of neglect and decay, have significance enough to merit its role as one of the principal threads in my story?

Part of its significance lies in that very fact, that it *is* a symbol of decay. Part lies in the very distant past, long before that story begins, when every spring of water and every stream born of those springs was the object of veneration by groups of primitive men who knew, as surely and instinctively as the birds and beasts still know, though most men have forgotten, that the water of those springs and streams was Life itself. The unfailing flow of that precious commodity, over which man had no control, could only be the bounteous manifestation of a divine power, indeed the very abode of divinity itself. And so the mind of man peopled the springs and streams with spirits, nymphs, goddesses – always female, for the notion of fertility was inevitably linked with the perennial flow of water. Then later, when man ceased to wander, and found the art of living always in one place, that place was determined by one of those springs or streams. Every village, not just in East Anglia but all over the world, owed its original location in part at least to the proximity or availability of water. Nymphs and sprites faded into the background, only vaguely remembered if at all, and considerations of practical common sense took their place.

As man became more and more settled, and needed to define the area of his settlement, practical considerations found another role for the stream. What better boundary-marker could there be? This aspect of the stream's significance is invisible on the ground today, but clear enough on the map. To the ten miles of our particular stream we must add a further seven miles of contributory streams. Of that total of seventeen miles, well over half constitute either county boundary, between Hertfordshire and Cambridgeshire, or parish boundaries separating the parishes of Reed, Barley, Great Chishill, Melbourn, Thriplow, Fowlmere, Shepreth and Foxton. At about the same time as the stream acquired this secondary role, the word 'common' also acquired a second meaning. It became common in that it belonged to no one in particular, but to everyone in general – everyone, that is, in one particular community. It was in fact the only thing, other than air, sunshine and rain, which was really and truly 'common'.

At least four of the villages listed above owe their existence to this one small stream-complex, and the account of the birth and growth of one of them, Foxton, is the second thread of my story. Rather more than a thread, it is a relatively wide and long expanse of tapestry. Long in that it extends over two thousand years. Wide in the sense that, though I may seem to tell only the story of one small village, I am in reality telling the story of many villages. All over East Anglia, the East Midlands, Central and Southern England – an area extending some eighty miles in all directions with Foxton at its geographical centre – there are hundreds and hundreds of villages. To tell the story of one is, in a way, to tell the story of them all. Of course they had, and still have, their differences and their individual characteristics. But the main stuff of which my tapestry is woven – early settlers, manors, serfdom, freemen, yeomen, buildings, crops, constables, enclosures etc. – is common to them all. I might have chosen to illustrate my theme from the records of all the villages; had I done so I would have lost in depth and continuity what I gained in width. I might have tried to deal with a hundred villages in the same detailed manner as I have dealt with Foxton and its immediate neighbours; that would have entailed another hundred years or so of research, and I do not think that I shall live that long. Moreover, the result would have been not one book but fifty, all very much alike. I chose to write about Foxton because I happen to live there; because, by pure chance, there is a remarkable wealth of documentary material available relating to Foxton; because unique archaeological opportunities in the immediate vicinity have presented themselves, again by pure chance. It so happened that, a few years ago, the River Rhee was properly dredged for the first time in its long history, and the dredger brought to light along with the mud enough relics of the past to fill a small museum. Not every village, of course, can boast a Roman villa, and my villa belongs geographically to Shepreth; but, as there were no parish boundaries when Roman villas were built, I have not hesitated to include it in my story. It was not chance which put the villa there; it was that same practical common sense to which I have already alluded.

From *The Common Stream*, Rowland Parker (Collins).

1 *Using not more than 70 words, explain, as fully as you can, the writer's first theme.* (10 marks)

2 *What was the writer's second theme? Why did he choose his particular*

*example, and how was he helped in his researches? Do not use more than
70 words.*   (10 marks)

Notice that neither of these questions uses the actual word *summary*,
but they are easily recognizable as summary questions by the number
of words allowed, and by the number of marks given for each. Comprehension questions can usually be answered in fewer words, and are
usually given 2, 3 or 4 marks each.

In this passage, the information for answering each question can be
easily identified; the information for the first is contained within the
first three paragraphs, while all the information you require to answer
the second question is in the last paragraph. Do not expect the material
to answer two summary questions to be always so conveniently divided;
information for both questions can be interspersed evenly throughout
the whole passage; you must then go through the passage once, collecting, in note form, the material for the first question, and then go
through a second time to collect material for the other question. (Or, if
you were astute, and had read through all your questions before you
started to answer them, you could save time by reading through once
only, collecting material for both questions simultaneously but under
separate headings.)

But once you have identified which questions call for summaries, the
techniques outlined in this chapter apply. Most comprehension answers,
as we shall see in the next chapter, can be answered straight off without
making a rough copy; but a good summary answer, because of the given
number of words, is always too complex to be written straight off
satisfactorily, even by the most experienced writer.

What we do notice here is that the first question covers about two
thirds of the original passage, the second only the last third, although
70 words are allowed for each. So the first summary will have to be
more concentrated than the second – assuming that the information is
fairly evenly spread.

So, when writing your rough notes, search for words which will sum
up the writer's argument; sometimes these will be words of your own,
but sometimes the best words are used by the writer, although they
often have to be adapted. For example, the notes for answering Question
1 could be:

1 (a) First theme 'Brook' (give course).
  (b) To most men insignificant, unnoticed, neglected – decay symbolic.
  (c) Primitive man venerated water – precious and divine.

(d) Later settled near water – utilitarian significance.

(e) Common property – boundary-marker (as now).

These notes could be developed into the following answer:

The writer's first theme is the ten-mile long nameless 'Brook' which rises south-east of Royston and flows to the River Rhee. To modern man it is insignificant, unnoticed and neglected; but this decay is symbolic. Primitive man venerated water as the source of life, precious and divine. Later, man settled near available water, which acquired utilitarian significance. It was common property, and, as it still is, a boundary-marker. (68 words)

Notes on this answer

1 The first sentence seems to be a waste of words, but the nameless stream must be identified exactly. (Try rewriting the first sentence to save words.)

2 Many of the words used in the summary were used by the writer, but in a different form. For example:

(a) 'no name' becomes 'nameless';

(b) 'how can such a miserable stream ... have significance enough ...' becomes 'insignificant';

(c) 'neglect' becomes 'neglected';

(d) 'symbol' becomes 'symbolic';

(e) 'the object of veneration' becomes 'venerated'.

This ability to adapt words is most useful in summary writing, and shows that you have made the concepts (and so the words) your own.

3 Some other words are used in both the original and summary in the same form, because they provide the best way to express the writer's ideas. It would be pointless to attempt to find other words for 'Brook', 'primitive', 'precious', 'divine', 'decay' etc.

4 Very few words in the summary are completely new: 'unnoticed', 'acquired', 'utilitarian' and 'property' are four – but the summary as a whole reads well on its own, and does not appear like a chopped-up version of the original. And all the main points of the writer's first theme have been mentioned.

The second question is a composite one, that is, it is really three questions in one. But it is still a summary question, because it is calling for the information given in the last paragraph, but in an abbreviated form. There are well over 400 words in that paragraph, and it must be reduced to not more than 70 words.

But not all the last paragraph is relevant to the question – or rather – questions. Re-read the question, and then the paragraph, and isolate the information that is not relevant to the question.

There is a long section in the middle of the paragraph about how the writer might have told his story, which is not relevant to the questions asked. So the substance of these three sentences – two of them very long – need not be included in the answer.

Furthermore, the information to answer the first question is contained in the first half of the paragraph (from the beginning to 'is common to them all'), and is elaborated by the image of the tapestry. Such an image is attractive and appropriate, because tapestries (e.g. Bayeux) often tell stories in vivid detail. But a summary should contain only the information asked for, and not be elaborated by figurative language, no matter how attractive. So all the words associated with the tapestry – 'thread', 'long', 'wide', 'stuff', 'woven' – must be omitted, and the question answered in plain and simple language.

Here is a first attempt at a sentence to answer this question:

The writer's second theme is the birth and growth, over more than 2,000 years, of the village of Foxton, which is typical of hundreds of other villages. (27 words)

This is quite good but it could be improved. In the first place, we could use the word 'origin' instead of 'birth', so as not to copy too much from the passage. Secondly, the sentence wastes words. The phrase 'of other villages' indicates that Foxton itself must be a village. So the four words 'of the village of' could be crossed out because they are superfluous, and superfluous words are to be avoided in a summary. We are left with:

The writer's second theme is the origin and growth, over more than 2,000 years, of Foxton, which is typical of hundreds of other villages. (24 words)

This is better. But it is not quite accurate. Why?

Foxton is typical of other villages, but not typical of villages everywhere – in Africa or Scotland, for example. The writer is quite specific about the geographical location of the hundreds of villages of which Foxton is typical: 'All over East Anglia, the East Midlands, Central and Southern England – an area extending some eighty miles in all directions with Foxton at its geographical centre' (26 words). But how can we reduce all this to make our sentence more accurate, but still use less than 30 words? To use any of those phrases – 'East Anglia', or 'the East Midlands', to describe all of them would be inaccurate. But when we read the second half of the sentence – 'an area extending some eighty miles in all directions with Foxton at its geographical centre' – and remember our geometry, the word 'radius' should come into our minds. Immediately we have an accurate and economical phrase – 'within a radius of eighty miles.' (6 words)

So the first sentence can be rewritten:

The writer's second theme is the origin and growth, over more than 2000 years, of Foxton, which is typical of hundreds of other villages within a radius of eighty miles. (30 words)

This is three words more than the original sentence, but much more accurate. But even those three words can be saved. The two words 'which is' are really unnecessary. So is the word 'other'. So we are left with a first sentence of 27 words, but much more accurate than the first attempt:

The writer's second theme is the origin and growth, over more than 2000 years, of Foxton, typical of hundreds of villages within a radius of eighty miles. (27 words)

This leaves us up to 43 words to answer the second half of the question: *Why did he choose his particular example, and how was he helped in his researches?*

The first part appears to be easy. He chose Foxton because he lived there. But this, by itself, is not quite accurate. He qualifies his choice by two further clauses: 'because, by pure chance, there is a remarkable wealth of documentary material available relating to Foxton'; and, secondly, 'because unique archaeological opportunities ... presented themselves'. Without those two conditions, he would not have chosen Foxton, even though he lived there. So that first bald sentence is not good enough; it must be taken further:

He chose Foxton for three fortuitous reasons: he lived there; the survival of many relevant documents; and the rich archaeological material provided by the dredging of the River Rhee. (29 words)

However, this still doesn't answer the second half of the question:

how was he helped in his researches? It is very common in the heat of an examination, to forget the second half of a question. We have 13 words left to answer the last question.

He was helped in three ways:
1 By the remarkable wealth of documentary material.
2 By the unique archaeological opportunities that presented themselves when the River Rhee was dredged.
3 By evidence from the Roman villa at Shepreth.

How can we get all this into 13 words? The first two have already been mentioned as reasons for his choice, so there is no need to elaborate on them again. Some such phrase as 'The last two' would be sufficient:

The last two helped his researches, as did evidence from the Roman villa at Shepreth. (15 words)

This is just too long. And the important thing about the Roman villa was that it was 'nearby'. The sentence could thus be rewritten:

The last two, with evidence from a nearby Roman villa, helped his researches. (13 words)

This is exactly the right length, so we can now copy out the complete answer:

The writer's second theme is the origin and growth, over more than 2000 years, of Foxton, typical of hundreds of villages within a radius of eighty miles. He chose Foxton for three fortuitous reasons: he lived there; the survival of many relevant documents; and the rich archaeological material provided by the dredging of the River Rhee. The last two, with evidence from a nearby Roman villa, helped his researches. (69 words)

Notes on this answer
1 Once again, it is arrived at by a process of gradually compressing the sentences in the answer, cutting out superfluous words.
2 At the same time, there is constant checking that the answer is strictly accurate, and, where necessary, adjustments are made.
3 A good vocabulary once again proved invaluable. Notice particularly how useful the words 'radius' and 'fortuitous' were.
4 Good punctuation was also useful. The sentence with the colon and

semi-colons could not be so neatly expressed without this punctuation.
5 The answer reads well when read on its own, it answers the question(s) completely and accurately, and it is written exactly within the limit of words.

We will end this chapter with an interesting and unusual summary question which comes from an actual examination paper. There is nothing in the question to suggest that it is an exercise in summary, but that is what it is; and if you identified it as a summary question, and answered it using the technique suggested in this chapter, you would be better able to tackle it.

The passage is a long one, and as well as the summary question it had 13 comprehension questions (not given in this chapter) for which a total of 35 marks were allowed. The summary question was allotted 15 marks and as it followed the comprehension questions, you would have read the passage several times by the time you came to answer it. Here you will have to read the passage separately, so allow yourself about 50 minutes to complete the questions. Tackle it yourself before you read the discussion on it.

Read the passage printed below and then answer the question that follows. (CAM)

(An advertisement in *The Times* offered adventure in Central Brazil. Peter Fleming was looking for adventure. He answered that advertisement which led to his taking part in 'an exploring and sporting expedition' to Central Brazil, where the explorer Colonel Fawcett had disappeared some years previously in an area that could only be reached from the headwaters of a tributary of the River Araguaya.)

Fleming and his companions reached Rio at sunset on the evening of 3 July 1932, to be met by a rush of photographers and by the man who was to be their leader. Captain Holman was a tall, thin man of about forty, described by Fleming as having 'a ragged moustache and phenomenally small ears, short mouse-coloured hair, and something of the camel in his gait'. He was a British resident of São Paulo, with allegedly unsurpassed experience of the interior.

Their aim was to leave at once for the interior, but in this they were frustrated by the customs officers who argued for six days about the expedition's baggage, which included a prodigious number of weapons, from sawn-off shotguns to revolvers, that had been considered necessary for survival. The wait naturally irked Fleming, but it also gave him a chance to observe Captain Holman at close quarters, and he was not much taken with what he saw, for Holman, although good at dealing with Brazilian bureaucrats, proved disconcertingly evasive when it came to discussing details of what the expedition was going to do. Then in São Paulo they were overtaken by a revolution, which threw the railways into chaos and halted the expedition for another five days. When they took to the road it was in a series of convulsive spurts and stops, their progress much hampered by revolutionary suspicions. At last the expedition got moving properly: two decrepit cars and a lorry were procured, and the party covered the last 130 miles to reach the River Araguaya in a single day of ferocious discomfort.

'The river ran slowly but strongly, making no sound at all.' On 30 July, accompanied by a motley crew seven strong, part Indian and part Brazilian, they set off downstream in a convoy of four boats. The crews kept the boats close to the banks, and a good deal of shooting was to be had every day, particularly for Holman and the men in the leading boat. Their choice of targets was regrettably catholic: almost every creature they spotted – fish, reptile, mammal or bird – drew fire. Meanwhile Fleming and his friends became increasingly worried about what would happen when they reached Bananal, where the Araguaya is joined by the Tapirapé, the tributary they had decided to explore. Captain Holman, whose talk was 'bland, irrelevant and enigmatic', side-stepped all their questions.

They found out soon enough. When they reached the Tapirapé, Holman came into the open and announced that he had no intention of proceeding up the smaller river. At once the expedition was divided. Fleming emerged as the leader of the faction in favour of pushing on. The rest were content to follow whatever lead Holman gave them. Tense, sarcastic arguments broke out. Under pressure, Holman agreed to make a quick journey up the Tapirapé, but, after one night in the jungle, to Fleming's unbounded elation, he suddenly announced that he himself was turning back; the rest, he said, could go on if they wanted, and he would await their return at Bananal. He disappeared downstream with one of the Indians in the smallest canoe.

Now, for the first time, the going became really strenuous. All day they paddled up the twisting river, which became ever shallower and was frequently blocked by overhanging branches, through which they had to cut their way. They decided to split into two parties, Fleming leading one party in a march on a compass-bearing across country, and the others continuing upstream. The days that followed were days of fierce physical strain, of considerable privation and risk, of real exploration. After some had dropped out, Fleming and two other men found themselves on their own in the middle of one of the biggest countries in the world, six weeks at least by water from the nearest point at which they could hope to get help. They had practically no equipment, they could scarcely communicate with the natives, and the Indians for whose territory they were aiming were reputed to be hostile. The food was practically exhausted, but the little party hacked their way on through the jungle. On the last day they fired patches of scrub so as to leave smoke-columns on which they could take back-bearings. By then they were constantly finding traces of Indians, and often their fires were answered by columns of smoke in the distance ahead. Several times they were drenched by thunderstorms, forerunners of the rains which would certainly put an end to their enterprise. There was no point in going on; reluctantly they returned to the river. Back at Bananal occurred the long-awaited confrontation with Captain Holman. Having been stuck for three weeks in that dreary place, he was exceedingly angry, and with a few last acrimonious exchanges the expedition finally disintegrated.

When Fleming came to write an account of all this in his famous book, *Brazilian Adventure*, he had one great difficulty: that of adequately portraying the foolishness and (as he saw it) downright dishonesty of Captain Holman. Had he made a direct attack, Holman would surely have sued him for libel or defamation, and yet if Fleming failed to show the man up he would be unable to explain why the expedition had broken up in the way it did. He solved the problem by a brilliant stroke. He saw Holman, in any case, as a split personality, and, instead of portraying him as one person, he showed him as two. The sensible, efficient long-term resident of São Paulo, the organizer whose skill and persistence got the expedition up-country through the chaos of revolution – this man he described as Captain J. H. Holman. But the boastful, evasive and cowardly poseur, whose presence ultimately proved disastrous to the expedition's chances of achieving any real success – this man he described as Major George Lewy Pingle, 'an American citizen holding, or claiming to hold, a commission in the Peruvian army'.

Only once, when he first introduced Major Pingle, did Fleming hint at the device which he had adopted. 'That is not his name,' he wrote. 'You can regard him as an imaginary character, if you like.' Thereafter he treated him as a real person, merely substituting 'Major Pingle' for 'Holman' whenever the man's behaviour became unwarrantably idiotic. Ninety-nine people out of a hundred would read the book without realizing what Fleming had done, but somebody exceptionally observant might notice that Holman – supposedly in charge of the whole enterprise – gradually fades from the picture as the expedition approaches the Araguaya, and never appears again. The device served its purpose admirably, for it scarcely detracted from the truth of the narrative, and it enabled the publishers' solicitors to pass the text for publication.

Duff Hart-Davis (adapted).

The actual advertisement in *The Times* that Peter Fleming answered was worded as follows:

> Exploring and sporting expedi-
> tion,   under   experienced
> guidance, leaving England June
> to explore rivers Central Brazil,
> if possible to ascertain fate of
> Colonel   Fawcett;   abundance
> game, big and small ; exceptional
> fishing;   ROOM   TWO   MORE
> GUNS; highest references ex-
> pected and given.
> Write Box X, *The Times*, E.C.4

The advertisement gives a partly fair and partly misleading picture of the sort of expedition that, in fact, it turned out to be under Captain Holman's leadership.

Write two short paragraphs to describe
1 *In your first paragraph, in what ways and to what extent the expedition fairly matched the hopes and expectations aroused by the wording of the advertisement,*
2 *In your second paragraph, in what ways and to what extent the expedition failed to satisfy these hopes and expectations.*
  Your complete answer to this question must not exceed 120 words, and you should avoid copying out lengthy phrases from the passage.
    (15 marks)(CAM)

This is not an easy question, and, I imagine, in the actual examination where it was set, it really sorted out the sheep from the goats. It emphasizes several of the qualities needed for good summary writing:

1 The need for concentration. There are many different factors to be held in your head while answering this question, and you cannot do this if you lose your concentration and let some of the factors slip out of your mind. It would be very easy to become confused when attempting to answer this question.

2 The need to read the passage slowly and carefully, so you understand what it is saying fully and clearly.

3 The need to read the question carefully so you make sure you answer exactly what you are asked to answer. Here the question is a long one, and includes the advertisement. You need to relate the question to the advertisement, to sort out exactly what you are asked to write.

4 The need for careful and efficient organization to collect the material for your two paragraphs. The time to write your answers to (1) and (2) is strictly limited, so you cannot afford to be inefficient and disorganized; this would only lead to incomplete and muddled answers.

One way to organize your notes to answer these two paragraphs would be as follows: on the left-hand side of your sheet of rough paper, in one column make a list of the various 'hopes and expectations aroused by the wording of the advertisement'. Then make two further columns to the right of this list, one headed 'fair' and the other headed 'misleading'. You can then go through the passage carefully and enter items under one of the two headings. You will then, under the two headings, have all the material you need to write your two paragraphs.

Your notes should look something like this, grouping related areas together:

Expectations of advert	Fair	Misleading
1 Exploring	Once the Tapirapé was reached there was some real exploring.	Any real exploring came about only because of Fleming's own initiative.
2 Sporting – abundant game and exceptional fishing	There was some sport on the Araguaya with plenty of game and fish for the leading boat.	No real sport for most members nor abundant game and exceptional fishing.

Expectations of advert	Fair	Misleading
3 Experienced guidance	Captain Holman efficient with bureaucrats – persistence and initiative got the expedition to River Araguaya, in spite of delays at customs and a revolution.	Captain Holman had no exploring experience – no leadership or planning so expedition disintegrated.
4 Ascertain fate of Colonel Fawcett	Expedition did reach the area near where Colonel Fawcett had disappeared.	No systematic attempt to ascertain fate of Colonel Fawcett.
5 Highest references		No evidence of references.

With the evidence for answering the two questions clearly and carefully organized in this way, it is then fairly easy to write the answers.

But even with the material clearly marshalled, it is still better to write rough copies of the answers first. You can then count the number of words and amend your sentences as necessary. This usually means finding ways of saving words. For example, the phrase 'came about' under the heading *Misleading* about *Exploring*, becomes the one word 'arose' in the finished version. A small but significant change, because with other similar changes, a considerable number of words can be saved so all the relevant evidence can be packed into the limited number of words.

Here are possible answers for the two paragraphs:

1 The expedition provided some real exploring once the Tapirapé was reached, and some sport on the Araguaya, with abundant game and fish for the leading boat. Captain Holman dealt efficiently with the bureaucratic customs officials, and, in spite of a revolution, his persistence and initiative got the expedition near where Colonel Fawcett disappeared. (53 words)

2 Any real exploration arose only through Fleming's own initiative, and, for most members, the expedition provided no real sport, nor abundant game and exceptional fishing. Captain Holman had no ex-

ploring experience. His lack of leadership and planning caused the expedition to disintegrate at the crucial time, so no systematic attempt was made to ascertain the fate of Colonel Fawcett. There is no evidence that references were exchanged. (67 words; total 120 words)

To sum up the points made in this chapter, good summary writing requires:

1 Complete concentration, because a good summary cannot be written with half-hearted attention.
2 Careful reading and complete understanding of the passage set.
3 Careful reading of the question, to make sure you do exactly what you are asked to do.
4 Efficient organization of your time.
5 Efficient collection, in rough form, of the material you need to answer the question.
6 Rewriting of a rough draft.
7 Constant alertness to find ways of saving words and make sure no superfluous words are included.
8 Final checking over of the finished answer, and writing in the number of words used (if asked to do so).

Examination practice

1 *Write a summary in good continuous prose of the following passage, taken from a Government publication, using not more than 120 words. State at the end of your summary the number of words you have used. The passage contains 342 words.* (16 marks)   (AEB)

Each year getting on for half a million boys and girls leave school and start work before they are 18. There are no very reliable statistics, but it would probably not be far off the mark to suggest that some 300,000 of these boys and girls receive little or no training from their employers.

This contrasts sharply with the practice of other countries in Western Europe where more, and more systematic, training is given for occupations which in this country are regarded as unskilled or semi-skilled. In Germany systematic training arrangements cover perhaps 70 per cent of the jobs into which young people go. In Sweden 70 per cent of young people take courses – lasting between two and four years – which include vocational education courses; only 10 per cent go straight into jobs and receive no vocational education at all.

The United Kingdom position is profoundly unsatisfactory. It is not easy to demonstrate the economic case in any readily quantifiable way because the failure to provide vocational preparation does not result immediately in shortages of workers lacking defined 'packages' of skills. But it seems certain that properly conceived vocational preparation would raise substantially the ability of many of these young workers. More important still, the experience of 'learning to learn' things relevant to work would help them to adapt to change more readily and therefore work more effectively throughout their lives. Proper training for young people would in fact raise the whole potential of the workforce. The importance of enabling workers to cope with change in a world of rapidly advancing technology does not need stressing. And there is the argument from social justice. As the State devotes more money to educating the more gifted up to and beyond university degree level, the gap between provision for them and provision for those who leave school at 16 to enter employment becomes wider.

Wherever one looks it becomes ever more clearly apparent that no lasting remedy can be achieved by tinkering with the existing training system: a radical revision will doubtless be needed.

Training Services Agency.

2 *The extract below is part of an account of the first invaders of these islands. Read it carefully and then answer the questions that follow.*
  (WEL)

It was between three thousand and two thousand-five-hundred years ago that the Celts or Gaels first appeared in Britain. They were tall, blue-eyed, flame-haired folk who had crossed Europe from the east and settled in the country which is now called France. They moved into Britain and Ireland, first in small bands and families and later in tribal armies until they had become the dominant racial strain in both islands.

The earlier peoples survived but were mostly driven into the western moors and hills. They figure in Celtic legends as the faeries or little people, elusive, mysterious and dangerous, who sometimes stole their neighbours' children or provided a bride for some good-humoured Celtic farmer. In such tales a recurrent feature is their dread of iron – the metal whose use the Celtic smiths introduced and which, forged into swords and chariots, gave their warriors their long ascendancy. Smelted in charcoal furnaces, it was made also into rotary lathes to make wheels, and into ploughs which, drawn by oxen, could break virgin soil too stiff for the hand hoes and small wooden ploughs of the past. This brought about a gradual increase in population which, it is estimated, rose during the Celtic occupation to around a quarter of a million. These iron users were probably the first people in Britain to create permanent fields and villages, mostly on the light clays of the south-east and in the south-west. At their zenith they may have occupied a sixth of the country.

The hereditary chieftains of the Celtic tribes seem to have had a love for beautiful things. They employed craftsmen whose graceful designs surpassed anything yet seen in the barbaric West. When they died their treasures were buried with them – bronze armour and helmets; embossed shields decorated with vivid enamels; golden torques, bracelets and brooches with which to fasten their tartan plaids; amber cups and hand-mirrors engraved with exquisite circular designs. Vanity was a characteristic of the Celts; a Greek traveller of the time describes them as smearing their fair hair with chalk-wash to make it still brighter and drawing it tightly back from their foreheads till they looked like hobgoblins. They used amazing colours, brightly dyed shirts with flowing patterns. They were boastful and threatening, he added, but their intellects were keen and they were quick to acquire knowledge.

They were also incorrigible fighters. They crowned Britain's hilltops, not with burial barrows and sun-temples but with vast earthwork castles with concentric ditches and ramparts. In the ancient Celtic ballads of Ireland, Wales and the Scottish Highlands pride of battle takes precedence over every other emotion.

In answering the following questions you are asked to use your own words as far as possible, to keep within the required number of words, and to use only information that is contained in the passage.

(a) *In what ways were the Celts efficient and strong people, the kind likely to be successful invaders and settlers? (Use between 80 and 100 words.)* (10 marks)

(b) *Show that the Celtic people also had an awareness of beauty. (About 60 words should be sufficient.)* (8 marks)

(c) *What do you learn of the people who inhabited these islands before the Celts? (Answer in two or three sentences.)* (2 marks)　　(WEL)

4 Comprehension

All examination boards have comprehension questions. This, of course, is to be expected, because understanding what you are reading is one of the basic requirements for proficiency in the English language. The comprehension questions test whether you have understood a passage (or passages) of moderate difficulty. All you have to do is to read the passage, then answer the questions that are about the passage. Nothing, it seems, could be simpler: yet few candidates gain high marks for the comprehension questions. Like so many simple tasks, it is all too easy to make mistakes.

Some boards now set multiple-choice questions on the passage – that is you are given a choice of four or five numbered answers and you have to choose the one that is correct, and fill in the number on an answer sheet, with no writing required at all. The emphasis here is on the actual comprehension of the passage, and not the writing of the answers. But most boards still require written answers to the comprehension questions. Both types of answer will be dealt with in this chapter, but you should study the whole chapter because it is all relevant.

The comprehension questions, like the summary, do not usually require you to generate any ideas of your own. All the material to answer the questions is in the passage itself. This, for some candidates, is the first difficulty; they are not prepared to give their full concentration to some topic which doesn't interest them. But complete concentration is the first requirement for understanding a passage. You must be prepared to go to a passage, give it a first exploratory reading to find out in general terms what it is about, and then give it a second, concentrated reading to attempt to understand exactly what it is saying.

You never know what the passages set for comprehension questions are going to be about. You might, if you keep an open mind, find something new and interesting. You must read with a fresh, open mind, being prepared to study each passage with a lively spirit of enquiry.

The following passage was set recently by an examining board. It is about a shop that sells second-hand jewellery, not a topic of interest to many people. But if you are prepared to give it your full attention (as you must do if you are to answer the questions correctly), you will find it is a most interesting and evocative piece of writing. Attempt to answer all the questions before you go on to read the discussion on the answers.

Read the following passage carefully and then answer the questions on it.
(20 marks)   (AEB)

Mor loved Tim's shop. The wooden shutters which covered the shop windows at night made it quite dark now within and in the dim light of the lamp it looked like some treasure cave or alchemist's den. Near the front there was a certain amount of order. Two
5 large counters, each in the form of a glass-topped cabinet, faced each other near to the street door. But beyond these the long shop became gradually chaotic. Loaded and untidy shelves, from floor to ceiling, ran round the three walls, well barricaded by wooden display cases of various types which stood often two or three deep,
10 in front of them. Between these, and in the rest of the available space, there were small tables, some of them also topped with glass and designed for display purposes. The more precious jewellery, such of it as was not behind the bars of the shop window, or hidden in the safes in the back room, was laid out in the glass-topped
15 cabinets, and ranged in fair order. Tim, when he tried, knew how to display his wares. He loved the stones, and treasured and displayed them according to his own system of valuation, which did not always accord with their market prices. This week, one of the cabinets was given over to a display of opals. Set in necklaces,
20 ear-rings, and brooches they lay, black ones and white ones, dusky ones flecked with blue or grey patches, and glowing water opals. The other cabinet was full of pearls, the real ones above, the cultured ones below, and worked golden objects. Mor had learnt a certain amount about stones during his long friendship with Tim.
25 This had been somewhat against his will, since for reasons which were not very clear to him, he rather disapproved of his friend's profession.

The front of the shop was orderly. But the cheaper jewellery which lay behind seemed to have got itself into an almost inex-

30   tricable mess. Within the squat glass-topped tables especially,
       ropes of beads were tangled together into a solid mass of multi-
       coloured stuff, and bold was the customer who, pointing to some
       identifiable patch of colour, said, 'I'll have *that* one.' Heaped
       together with these were clips and ear-rings, their fellows often
35   irrevocably missing, brooches, bracelets, buckles, and a miscellany
       of other small adornments. Tim Burke was not interested in
       the cheap stuff. He seemed to acquire his stock more or less by
       accident in the course of his trade and dispose of it without
       thought, to such determined individuals as were prepared to
40   struggle for what they wanted, often searching the shop from end
       to end to find the second ear-ring or the other half of a buckle.

       From *The Sandcastle*, Iris Murdoch (Chatto and Windus)

*1 Explain in your own words the effect of the lamplight on the interior of
   the shop.*   (3 marks)
2 What do you learn about the layout and furniture of the shop?
   (3 marks)
*3 What impressions have you gathered from the passage of Tim's short-
   comings?*   (3 marks)
*4 In your own words say what difficulties the intending buyer of cheaper
   jewellery has to face.*   (3 marks)
5 What do you understand by the following expressions?
   (a) a miscellany of other small adornments (lines 35–6)
   (b) determined individuals prepared to struggle (lines 39–40)
        (4 marks)
6 Give a word or phrase of similar meaning to each of four *of the following
   as used in the passage:*
   chaotic (line 7) barricaded (line 8) available (line 10)
   accord (line 18) worked (line 23) squat (line 30)   (4 marks)   (AEB)

One good general instruction for studying the passage set for comprehension is to read it in the spirit in which it was written. In the
chapter on composition, we saw that there are many different kinds of
writing: descriptive, informative, narrative, humorous, argumentative
etc. The passages set for comprehension can also be in any type of
writing; in fact, with those boards that set more than one piece of writing,
the passages are purposely different. You must be willing to switch your
attention to be able to read each passage as it was intended to be read.
One good way to do this is to imagine you are reading aloud to someone
slightly younger than yourself. Your first reading should be the ex-

ploratory reading; but on the second reading, imagine you have an interested listener, so you have to read the passage bringing out its main points – its humour, or its information, or its argument. Of course, in the examination room, you cannot read the passage aloud; but it is possible to read silently as if you were reading to make the meaning explicit to someone else. You are then more likely to make the meaning of the passage explicit to yourself. This is important because, with many passages, it is not only the surface meaning of the words which you have to understand, but also the meaning implicit in the words, the meaning between the lines.

This passage is chiefly descriptive. Iris Murdoch, the author, obviously enjoyed describing Tim's shop, and also, to a lesser degree in this passage, Tim himself. (It comes from her novel *The Sandcastle*.) When you are reading the passage you must savour this description, enjoying the richness and the detail. You are then more likely to answer the questions successfully, because the examiner is in fact testing your ability to appreciate the quality of the description. For example, if the passage is a humorous one, at least some of the questions will test whether you have appreciated the humour. Or if the passage is a scientific or informative one, some of the questions will test if you have accurately picked up the information given. Here, most of the questions are testing if you have 'pictured' the shop in your own mind; if you have, then you can be said to have comprehended the passage: if you have not, then you cannot have really read the passage, even though your eyes had taken in all the words.

Here are possible answers to the questions, with comments:

1 This question can be answered entirely from evidence in the second
   sentence: 'The wooden shutters . . . like some treasure cave or
   alchemist's den.' Notice, however, that the question asks you to
   explain *in your own words*; so to quote directly from the sentence
   would not gain you marks. There are really three parts to the effect
   of the lamplight that you have to explain:
   (a) the shop was quite dark even in daylight because of the wooden
        shutters; and the dim light of the lamp made the shop look like
   (b) 'some treasure cave'; or
   (c) 'alchemist's den'.
   'Alchemist' is possibly the only word not familiar to you: an alchemist
was the medieval forerunner of a chemist who, in particular, tried to
turn non-precious metals into gold. He was a kind of magician working

in what we would call a laboratory. You don't have to find any new words for 'shutters' or 'shop', but you do for the phrases 'treasure cave' and 'alchemist's den'.

When you are asked to *use your own words* you must also use your common sense: there are always some basic words which you must retain, so there is no need to attempt to find synonyms for 'shop' and 'shutters' in this question. Notice, as well, you are asked to *explain*, not just put the words of the passage into your own words. And to explain the 'effect of the lamplight' you have to use your imagination. This is what was meant earlier by reading **not only the surface meaning**, but also the **implications**. Here, if you read imaginatively, you realize that the effect of the lamplight was not to light everything up clearly, but only to highlight certain bright spots in the general dimness.

So a possible answer could read:

Because of the shutters, the shop was quite dark inside, even in daylight, so the effect of the lamplight was to highlight certain bright spots in the general dimness, making the place look like some secret store of precious items, or the laboratory of some magician.

This answer highlights the quality of Iris Murdoch's writing; she's said all this much more effectively in far fewer words! Another point, however, is also highlighted by this answer: the questions are sometimes not quite as obvious as you might think at first glance. Even though all the material for answering this question is contained in one sentence, you need to think carefully about both the sentence, and the question, before framing your answer. Otherwise, you would find yourself gaining only 1 or 2 marks, and not the full 3 allowed, because you haven't done exactly, and fully, what the question asked you to do.

2 This question is also about the description, but rather more factual than imaginative; and the material to answer it is scattered through the passage, not neatly contained in one sentence. There is also quite a lot of material, so it is not easy to gather it together in one fairly short answer, which need not, of course, be just one sentence.

You are asked to answer on two points: the *layout* and the *furniture*. The two points are related, but not the same; so you would not gain full marks if you wrote about one and not the other. Here is a possible answer:

Near the door at the front of the shop, two large glass-topped cabinets, which faced each other, acted as counters. The three walls of the long shop had shelves from floor to ceiling. In front of these shelves were display cases, often two or three deep, and every other available space was filled with small tables, some with glass tops. The front of the shop was orderly, but it became more chaotic the further you penetrated from the door.

This seems a long answer for just 3 marks, but you must not expect the number of marks to work out proportionately to the number of words you use in each answer. What you must do is to make sure you answer, as briefly as possible, every part of the question. Here, the layout is given in some detail, which cannot be summarized; so your answer must give the details.

But here again, you could not give an adequate answer if you had not visualized the details in your own mind, and to do that, you need to have read the passage with close attention.

3 This question concerns the description of a character. Notice, again, that this is a question not only about factual information, but about *impressions you have gathered*: in effect, you are being told to read between the lines. Note, however, that this is not a general question about Tim; it is about his *shortcomings*.

   (a) 'the long shop gradually became chaotic'. Although this is a descriptive detail about the shop, it also tells us something about Tim; he only took trouble to keep the front part of the shop in a certain amount of order!

   (b) 'Tim, when he tried, knew how to display his wares.' The clause 'when he tried' implies that he didn't always take the trouble to try, which is another of his shortcomings.

   (c) 'the cheaper jewellery . . . was in . . . an almost inextricable mess . . . Tim was not interested in the cheaper stuff . . . acquired it by accident . . . disposed of it without thought.' As the cheaper jewellery was part of Tim's livelihood, his disregard for it must be considered as a shortcoming.

How can all this evidence be gathered together in a reasonably short answer? But remember the question was not a factual one. It might be as well to re-read it, to see exactly what it is asking: *What impressions have you gathered from the passage of Tim's shortcomings?*

A possible answer could be:

As a seller of jewellery, Tim was not very efficient or businesslike:

only the front part of his shop was fairly orderly, the rest chaotic; he did not always take the trouble to display the jewels to the best advantage; and his cheaper jewellery, in which he had no interest, was in an almost inextricable mess, and he acquired and sold it without thought.

This, again, is a fairly long answer, but it needs to be to get the full 3 marks. A general answer with no detail, such as 'As a seller of jewellery Tim was not very efficient or businesslike' would probably gain only half a mark, and this is the kind of answer that many candidates give. It is, in one way, a correct answer, so why, you might ask, doesn't it get full marks? The answer is, that to gain full marks for the answers to comprehension questions, you must give the *evidence* for your general statements, even if they are *impressions* you have gathered.

Some candidates answering this question might put the following point as one of Tim's shortcomings: 'He displayed his wares according to his own system of valuation, which did not always accord with their market value', arguing that as selling jewels was his profession, not to give them their proper market value was a shortcoming. But these candidates would not have read the passage carefully enough. Nowhere does it say that Tim did not *sell* his jewels for their true market value; he only *displayed* them according to his own valuation. So this is doubtful evidence about his shortcomings, because there is nothing wrong (perhaps the opposite) in having his own system of valuation, so long as he still knew the market prices. So if this is an impression you have gathered, you have gathered it from not reading closely enough. And you will not gain marks for giving impressions which bear no relation to what is actually said in the passage. This is why your reading must be objective, careful and close, and not a quick glance over, getting a hazy, subjective notion of what the passage is about. Your appreciation of it must be complete and exact.

Notice the punctuation used in this answer: the use of the colon, then the semi-colons, enables the general point to be made, and then the three examples clearly distinguished.

4 This question once again asks you to answer *in your own words*. All the evidence is in the last paragraph. There are two points that have to be made:
(a) 'the cheaper jewellery . . . had got itself into an almost inextricable mess . . . tangled together into a solid mass.'
(b) 'their fellows often irrevocably missing . . . searching the shop from end to end'.

Here is a possible answer:

The buyer of cheaper jewellery had to face two difficulties: the first was that the cheaper jewellery was in complete disorder, so the buyer had to disentangle the wanted ornament; secondly, some vital piece of the ornament was often missing, so the buyer had to look all over the shop to try to find it.

This is a much more straightforward question, asking for factual information other than impressions or implications. Note, once again, how important good punctuation is in this answer: the use of the colon and the semi-colon enables the answer to be perfectly controlled in one long sentence.

5   This is another straightforward question. But when asked to give the meaning of expressions, what is meant is their meaning *as used in the passage*. So you must go back to the passage, and read each expression in its context.

In (a) there are really two words that need explaining: *miscellany* and *adornments*. So an answer such as:

---

5 (a) A mixture of other small pieces of jewellery

---

could gain full marks.

In (b) it is not so easy to isolate the two words that would gain the marks; the whole expression needs explaining, once again, as it is used in the passage. A possible answer could be:

---

5 (b) People who knew what they wanted and were willing to make a
           particular effort.

Note that both the answers could be put into the passage in place of the words we have been asked to explain, and the sense could remain the same.

Note, as well, that the questions are numbered 5 (a) and (b), so the answers are numbered 5 (a) and (b).

6   As the six words are not numbered, in order to make your answers clear, it would be best to write out your four words on separate lines, with your equivalent word or phrase on the same line. Note that you are asked for *a word or phrase of similar meaning to each of* four *of the following as used in the passage*. The last five words are important –

as used in the passage; the question is not testing if you know what the words mean, but if you have understood how they are used in the passage. This means you must go back to the passage and re-read the sentence in which they appear very carefully. Very often, when words are chosen in this way, they are not words which are particularly unusual; but they are often used in an unusual way.

You are asked to give answers to only *four* words; so give only four. If you answer all six, the examiner will mark the first four and cross out the last two because you haven't done what you were asked to do. So the best plan is for you to answer all six in rough – if you can – and then choose the four you think are best, and copy those out on your examination paper.

Here is how all six could be answered:

chaotic	= without order
barricaded	= shut off
available	= usable
accord	= agree
worked	= engraved or modelled
squat	= short and small

Notice that each of the equivalent words or phrases could be put in the sentence in which the original word is used *without altering the sense*. This means that the same grammatical form of the word must be used. For example, the word 'accord' as used in the passage, is a verb:

His valuation did not always accord with the market value.

Therefore the equivalent must also be a verb:

His valuation did not always agree with the market value.

So a noun, such as *agreement*, would not be considered correct.

In a question such as this, do not do more than you need to do. You are asked to give a *word* or *phrase*, so give a *word* or *phrase*, and don't go off into long explanations. You won't gain any extra marks. Notice that 4 marks are given for this question, and you can gain full marks by writing down four words or phrases and nothing more.

To summarize the points made in the answers to the questions on this passage:

1 You must read the passage twice before you attempt to answer any of the questions: the first reading being an exploratory reading to find out what it is about; the second a careful reading, appreciating

the style of writing, and understanding the implications as well as the meaning. This cannot be done with only half-hearted attention.

2   You must read each question carefully, and make sure your answer does exactly what the question asks you to do.

3   Give evidence in support of general statements.

4   When asked to *use your own words*, make sure you do so; but at the same time realize there are usually some basic words which appear in the passage which you must also retain.

5   If you are asked to give *one word or phrase*, give one word or phrase, and don't give a long explanation.

6   Number your answers exactly as the questions are numbered. So if the questions are numbered 1, 2 (a) (b) (c), 3 etc., number your answers 1, 2 (a) (b) (c), 3 etc., and not (a), (b), (i) (ii) (iii), (c) etc. If the subsections of a question are not numbered, make sure it is quite clear to the examiner which parts of the question you are answering.

Here is another comprehension test: this time the passage is a piece of narrative, with dialogue, and the questions are much more exact, generally needing much shorter answers. Two of the questions, in fact, are of the multiple choice type.

However, the technique for answering these questions is the same: read the passage through once to explore what it is about; then read it a second time to understand exactly what is going on, and how the different characters react to the situation.

Read the instructions carefully too, and note that a clear distinction is made between those questions where you should *use your own words*, and those where you should *quote words from the passage*.

Attempt to answer all the questions before you go on with the discussion on the answers.

Read this passage carefully and then answer the questions that follow, using, where possible, your own words. Where you are asked to quote (and this is indicated by an asterisk), take care to quote only the appropriate word or words.   (SCOT)

Private Roth was completely absorbed in the bird. Each time it would open its tiny beak and try to bite his finger, he would feel a protective pang. Its entire body would flutter and vibrate from the effort, and yet there was hardly any pressure at all on his finger.

5   Despite himself he would bring the bird up to his nose and sniff it,
    touching his lips against its soft feathers. Its eyes were so bright
    and alert. Roth had fallen in love with the bird immediately and all
    the frustrated affection he had stored for months seemed to pour
    out towards it. He fondled it and examined its injured wing
10 tenderly. And back of it, not quite conscious, he was also enjoying
    the interest of the men who had crowded around him to look. For
    once he was the focus of attention.

    He could not have picked a worse time to antagonize Croft.

    Sergeant Croft was sweating from the labour of making the
15 stretcher alone: when he finished, all the difficulties of the patrol
    were nagging at him again. And deep within him his rage was alive
    again, flaring. Everything was wrong, and Roth played with a bird,
    while nearly half the platoon stood about watching.

    His anger was too vivid for him to think. He strode across the
20 hollow, and stopped before the group around Roth.

    'Jus' what do you men think you're doin'?' he asked in a low
    strained voice.

    They all looked up, instantly wary. 'Nothin',' one of them
    muttered.

25 'Roth!'

    'Yes, Sergeant?' His voice quavered.

    'Give me that bird.'

    Without a word, Roth passed it to him, and Croft held it for a
    moment. He could feel the bird's heart beating like a pulse against
30 his palm. Its tiny eyes darted about frantically, and Croft's anger
    worked into his fingertips. It would be the simplest thing to crush
    it in his hand; it was no bigger than a stone. He didn't know
    whether to smooth its soft feathers or smash it in his fingers.

    'Can I have it back, Sergeant?' Roth pleaded.

35 The sound of his voice, already defeated, worked a spasm
    through Croft's fingers. He heard a little numbly the choked squeal
    of the bird, the sudden collapsing of its bones. It thrashed power-
    lessly against his palm, and the action aroused him to nausea and
    rage again. He felt himself hurling the bird away over the other
40 side of the hollow, more than a hundred feet. Then his knees were
    left trembling.

    For a long instant no one said anything.

    And then the reaction lashed about him. Ridges stood up in a
    fury, advanced towards Croft. 'What you doin'? . . . . why'd you

45 do that to the bird? What do ya mean. . . . ?'
        Goldstein, shocked and genuinely horrified, was gaping at him.
    'How can you do such a thing? What harm was that bird doing
    you? Why did you do it? It's like. . . . like. . . .' He searched for the
    most outrageous crime. 'It's like killing a baby.'
50   Croft, unconsciously, retreated a step or two. He was startled
    momentarily into passiveness by the force of their response.
        From *The Naked and the Dead*, Norman Mailer (André Deutsch)

Questions

  1 (a) Which two things about the bird made Roth sympathetic towards
        it?   (2 marks)
   *(b) Roth is a caring man. Which word in the first paragraph shows
        clearly that he has had no outlet for his feelings?   (1 mark)
  2 'For once he was the focus of attention' (line 12)
     (a) What is meant by 'he was the focus of attention'?   (1 mark)
     (b) What does 'for once' tell us about the kind of person Roth really
        was?   (1 mark)
   *(c) Later on in the passage there are other clues to the character of
        Roth. Quote <u>one</u> of these and say what it tells you about him.
        (2 marks)
  3 Which one of the following definitions is closest in meaning to 'antagon-
        ize' (line 13)?   (1 mark)
            interrupt
            irritate
            contradict
            address
            infuriate
  4 Sergeant Croft is in a terrible temper and the third paragraph (lines
    14–18) suggests several reasons for this.
    Using your own words, write down <u>two</u> of these reasons.   (2 marks)
  5 (a) What is meant by 'His anger was too vivid for him to think'?
        (line 19)   (1 mark)
     (b) What does 'strode' (line 19) tell us about how Croft moved on this
        occasion?   (1 mark)
  6 (a) Why, apart from the fact that Croft was angry, were the men
        'instantly wary' (line 23) when the Sergeant addressed them?
        (1 mark)
     (b) How is their 'wariness' conveyed by the writer in the very next
        sentence?   (1 mark)

(c) *Why is there an exclamation mark after 'Roth' (line 25)?* (1 mark)

7 ★*In the paragraph beginning, 'Without a word' (line 28), the writer clearly wants us to feel sympathy for the bird. Quote two expressions which show how he tries to enlist our sympathy here.* (2 marks)

8 *'For a long instant no one said anything' (line 42). Was this mainly because the soldiers were*
    (i) *all terrified of Croft's temper?*
    (ii) *shocked by what he had done?*
    (iii) *afraid of what he would do to them next?*
    (iv) *indifferent to what happened to the bird?*
    Write down (i), (ii), (iii) or (iv). (1 mark)

9 *Two soldiers, Ridges and Goldstein, reacted to the killing of the bird.*
  (a) *In your own words, describe how each soldier felt about what had been done.* (2 marks)
  (b) *By examining how they addressed Croft, show any differences between them as people.* (2 marks)

10 *Why did Croft retreat a step or two (line 50)?* (1 mark)

11 *There is some evidence in the passage that Croft is not altogether a heartless monster.*
  ★(a) *Quote an expression that shows this.* (1 mark)
  (b) *In your own words, explain exactly what this expression proves.* (1 mark)

In this passage, as in the previous one, you must not only read the words and understand them, but also respond to what is happening. Nearly all the words and language used are extremely simple; but to comprehend the passage fully, you must *feel* within yourself what the characters felt. So comprehension is not only a matter for the head, but also for the heart. The incident with the baby bird is vividly described by the author, and the reactions of the different soldiers acutely observed. Nearly all the questions are testing if you have responded in the way the author intended.

Here are possible answers:

---

1 (a) Roth was sympathetic towards the bird because it was hungry and because it had a broken wing.

Unless you are told otherwise, it is better to answer in complete sentences. Notice the first half of the sentence comes from the question itself. The two reasons for Roth's sympathy are given *in your own words*.

There are other possible reasons, such as, for example, just that the bird was 'tiny'; but the two given are the best, because they are both qualified in the passage by an extra comment: 'he would feel a protective pang' when the bird opened its tiny beak and tried to bite his finger – i.e. indicating that it was hungry; and he examined its injured wing 'tenderly'. When there is a choice, pick the best examples to answer the questions. But when asked for *two things*, give two and not more.

(b) 'frustrated'.

Here you are not asked to give any reason or comment, so don't give any. The full mark is given for the one word quoted from the first paragraph. There is no other word that shows clearly that Roth has had no outlet for his feelings. Note that quotation marks are used because the word is quoted from the passage.

---

2 (a) Many of the men had gathered round Roth, watching what he was doing with the bird.

Once again, the answer is one short sentence. The two points that need to be brought out are that the men were 'round' Roth, and were 'looking' at what he was doing.

(b) The use of the phrase 'for once' tells us that Roth was usually a quiet and retiring person.

This is a good example of a question that needs some reading between the lines. It is only by implication that we come to realize, from the passage, the kind of person Roth was.

(c) 'Without a word, Roth passed it to him.' This shows that Roth was usually quiet and obedient.

This is another question that can be answered correctly only if you have understood the implications of the words. The word *clue* in the question seems to indicate that you have to interpret the words. Notice the quotation marks again.

There are other possible words, e.g. 'His voice quavered' or ' "Can I have it back, Sergeant?" Roth pleaded.'

3 Infuriate

This is a multiple choice question. One way to make your choice is to eliminate those words which are obviously wrong. 'Address', 'contradict' and 'interrupt' could be crossed out fairly quickly, leaving you with the choice between 'irritate' and 'infuriate'. As used in the passage, 'irritate' is too weak, which leaves you with the one possible word. Notice the question does not ask for the word with the *same meaning*, but the one *closest in meaning*.

4 Two reasons why Sergeant Croft is in a terrible temper are that he had had no help in making the stretcher, and that nothing was going right for him.

'All the difficulties of the patrol were nagging at him' and 'Roth played with a bird' and 'nearly half the platoon stood about' are three further reasons, but these are not so easy to give *in your own words*.

5 (a) He was in such a bad temper that he couldn't think reasonably.

The general directions tell you to *use your own words*, where possible. It is difficult to give a correct answer without using the word 'think', so it is retained.

(b) 'Strode' tells us that Croft moved firmly and with decision.

This is another question which requires you to have entered into the spirit of the piece and to have a clear picture of the scene. 'To stride' can denote a quiet, peaceful action; but not as used in this passage.

6 (a) The men were wary because they suddenly realized they had been standing round doing nothing when Croft had been busy.
(b) The word 'muttered' shows the man was too nervous to speak out loudly and clearly.
(c) There is an exclamation mark after 'Roth' to indicate that Croft speaks sharply and decisively.

These are all questions that can be answered correctly if you have read closely. It is only through the implications of the words that you can realize that the men were wary because after Croft's question: 'Jus' what do you men think you're doin'?' they realize they had been standing around doing nothing when Croft had been 'sweating from the labour of making the stretcher alone'. So the word 'muttered' is more than descriptive; it also conveys the men's uneasiness; and there must be an exclamation mark after 'Roth!' to show the sharpness of the Sergeant's reaction.

---

7 'He could feel the bird's heart beating like a pulse against his palm' and 'Its tiny eyes darted about frantically.'

There are several other expressions that could be quoted, but these are the two best.

---

8 (ii) This is another multiple choice question, and (ii) is the only correct answer to give the reaction of the men.

---

9 (a) Ridges was angry and unable to understand why Croft had been so cruel.
Goldstein was filled with horror and was stupefied by the cruel action.

This is another question which needs a complete understanding of the tension of the scene. Notice that you are required to *use your own words*; it is not easy to find a word or phrase in place of the word 'shocked' as applied to Goldstein.

(b) Ridges' use of 'doin' ', 'why'd' and 'ya', and his broken sentences, seem to indicate he was not very well educated or articulate. Probably working-class.
Goldstein does not use any form of dialect, so he is, perhaps, better educated and of middle-class origin.

Notice that the question asks you to examine *how they addressed Croft*, rather than what they said. This again is an inference question, not what you are actually told. Other inferences could be drawn: that Ridges was quick-tempered and not very bright; that Goldstein was humane, reasoning and intelligent.

---

10 Croft retreated a step or two because he was, for a moment, shocked by the violence of the men's reactions.

It would not be true to say that Croft was 'frightened' – there is no evidence for that – but he was 'startled', and you have to find your own word for that reaction.

11 (a) 'He didn't know whether to smooth its soft feathers.'
  (b) This expression proves that the more gentle reaction to the
       baby bird did occur to Croft, and had he not been so angry, this
       is what he would have done.

There is more evidence in the passage that Croft is not altogether a
heartless monster. That he was 'making the stretcher alone', is not
sufficient evidence, because we are not told the circumstances for this.
'He heard a little numbly the choked squeal of the bird' could be,
because it does show he reacted to the pain of the bird. 'Then his knees
were left trembling' could also indicate that he reacted to his cruel
action. But you are asked to give only one expression, and that given is
the best.

To summarize the points made in the answers to this question:

1 This test is an excellent example of how you cannot read the passage
  in a half-hearted way and then expect to be able to answer the
  questions accurately. Many of the questions don't make sense unless
  you have felt as well as understood what is going on in this incident.
  This is why your reading of the passage must be thorough and
  careful, with an appreciation of the depth of meaning. This passage
  demonstrates that comprehension is not so much a test of
  understanding long words and difficult language – nearly all the words
  and sentences in this piece are short and simple – but of reading with
  sympathy.
2 Never write more in any answer than you are asked to do, but if
  you are not told otherwise, answer in complete sentences.
3 If you are quoting words from the original passage – that is in a
  question where you do not have to use your own words – then put
  all direct quotations in quotation marks.
4 If there are several choices for an answer, give the best examples,
  and only as many as you are asked to give. Don't list them all, and
  expect the examiner to choose the best; you have to make the choice.
5 Make sure you number your answers exactly as the questions are
  numbered. The subdivisions in the questions here are important,
  so they must be completely clear in your answers.
6 Check over your work carefully after you have finished, to make sure
  you have made no mistakes. Errors of spelling, punctuation and
  grammar can all lose marks in comprehension answers (apart from
  the multiple choice type of answer).

7 Where you have a multiple choice question, read the question and all
   the alternatives carefully, and select your answer by a process of
   elimination until you are left with the only possible alternative.

The next passage is different in two ways: first of all, it is not descriptive or narrative writing, but a piece of popular science, giving
information, ideas and theories; secondly, all the questions on this
passage are of the multiple choice type. Even if your board does not
usually set multiple choice questions, you would be wise to study this
section, because there are other lessons to learn about comprehension,
and, as we have seen, multiple choice questions can sometimes appear
amongst questions demanding written answers.

Read the passage twice, and then attempt to answer the questions
yourself before reading on. There are eleven questions, so on a piece of
paper write the numbers 1 to 11, and then, against each, write the
correct letter for each answer.

*Read the following passage carefully, then read the directions after
it.*   (LOND)

   In territorial animals, it may be said that aggression, which
   originally served the function of ensuring that the animal could
   compete with its neighbour in the struggle for food, has now come
   to serve the function of putting a distance between itself and its
5 neighbour. There can be no doubt that man, also, is a territorial
   animal. Even in circumstances so far removed from the primitive
   as contemporary Western civilization, the countryside is demarcated by fences and hedges many of which carry notices stating that
   'Trespassers will be prosecuted'; and the entry of our houses by
10 unauthorized persons is resented as much as the loss of any
   property with which they may abscond. On a national scale, the
   invasion of the homeland by an enemy evokes a more passionately
   aggressive response than does a battle with the same foe on territory which belongs to neither.
15   Like other animals, man also reacts badly to overcrowding.
   Those of us who live in towns have learned to accommodate
   ourselves to some degree to the kind of congestion which seems to be
   an inevitable sequel of urbanization; but, the closer we are packed,
   the more easily resentful of each other do we tend to become. It is
20 probably on this account that many people find life in cities irritating and exhausting, since they are compelled to control aggressive
   impulses which arise solely as a result of overcrowding. It is also

probable that it is because of the wider spacing between individuals which is usual in the countryside that rural folk are
25 less tense, more neighbourly, and often better mannered than their
urban counterparts.

Directions

*Read the passage carefully and then answer the questions. Each question
has five suggested answers. Select the best answer to each question and
mark the answer sheet accordingly.* (LOND)

1 *The expression 'contemporary
Western civilization', as used
in line 7, is best explained as
the way of life*
A *experienced by workers in a
modern capitalist society*
B *depicted in modern American
films about the Wild West*
C *experienced in districts where
modern progress has wiped
out primitive life*
D *depicted in books about
wealthy people*
E *experienced in typical districts
of modern Europe and
America*

2 *The word 'abscond', as used
in line 11, is best explained as*
A *go away secretly*
B *escape from custody*
C *avoid lawful arrest*
D *hide away temporarily*
E *make a profit*

3 *According to the first paragraph,
the most obvious distinguishing
mark of the territorial animal is*
A *striving for food*
B *fear of burglary*
C *dislike of war*
D *interest in fighting*
E *resentment against intruders*

4 *The expression 'learned to
accommodate ourselves' (lines
16–17) means that we have
discovered how to*
A *find sufficient living space*
B *adapt our natural attitudes*
C *adjust our everyday needs*
D *make a comfortable home*
E *live in congested neighbour-
hoods*

5 *The expression 'an inevitable
sequel of urbanization'
(lines 18) is best explained as*
A *an essential part of town life*
B *a final development of the
overcrowding in cities*
C *an unavoidable result of the
development of cities*
D *a necessary conclusion of the
overcrowding in cities*
E *a logical by-product of
town-planning*

6 *According to the sentence in
lines 19–22, the reason that
many people find life in cities
irritating and exhausting is
that they are forced to*
A *keep away from others with
whom they may feel a sudden
impulse to quarrel*

B behave aggressively because of impulsive feelings caused by overcrowding

C live too close to others, without the benefit of open rural spaces

D restrain the urges prompted by resentment caused by overcrowding

E check all their inner feelings because their living conditions are overcrowded

7 The writer suggests that city life is exhausting because it frequently forces people to

A behave badly towards other people

B be active for longer periods of time

C ward off would-be trespassers

D keep aggressive urges in check

E compete more strongly for promotion

8 Which one of the following statements best summarizes the main content of the second paragraph?

A Man is happiest when he lives alone.

B Country life makes people more polite and happier in their lives.

C In cities, overcrowding causes resentment through frustration of natural instincts.

D City dwellers learn how to control their primitive impulses.

E Urbanization is inevitable in the future but leads to overcrowding.

9 The best evidence to support the author's main argument is contained in the fact that

A town dwellers have to some extent become adapted to congestion

B congestion follows inevitably from the development of towns

C civilized man does not have to fight for food

D invasion of national territory is particularly fiercely resisted

E intruders steal from houses in a civilized society

10 The chief reason given in the passage for regarding man as an animal is that he

A cannot control his aggressive impulses

B behaves in a savage fashion towards others

C has failed to develop as a civilized being

D shares certain forms of animal behaviour

E has evolved few admirable qualities

11 The main purpose of the passage is to

A show how modern man differs from primitive man

B explain some of the behaviour of city dwellers

C show that town life is inferior to country life

D *explain why most people*   **E** *prove that civilization is*
    distrust each other   *beneficial to man*

This passage needs to be read coolly and carefully. A hurried reading, skimming over the surface, will not reveal the meaning. There are several quite long and difficult sentences in which the sense can easily be lost. There are also several fairly difficult words – 'territorial', 'demarcated', 'contemporary', 'abscond', 'urbanization', 'accommodate', for example – which need careful consideration if the meaning of the passage is to be fully understood.

There is another danger with a passage which gives ideas or theories, particularly if they are controversial. It is always possible that you have some ideas of your own; here, for example, on the comparative benefits of living in the town or in the country. But you must not let your own opinions cloud your understanding of what the author of the passage is saying; the questions will all be on what the author is saying about the topic, not what you think.

Another difficulty emerges with the questions on this passage. Some of them are on the individual parts of the passage, but many of them are testing whether you have understood the main drift and argument of the paragraphs, and also of the passage as a whole. This means that you must have a clear head, to be able to hold in your mind the ideas or theories that are being put forward. You cannot keep going back to re-read the whole passage, or even a paragraph. That is why your second reading should be slow and thorough, so you can then understand exactly what the author is saying.

Multiple choice questions are easier in one way, because you don't have to do any writing to answer them. But in other ways they are more difficult. First of all, the passages you are given to read are usually longer in their total length than those set for written answers, so there is more to remember while answering the questions. Secondly, the alternative answers themselves are often quite long, and because they are all so close to the correct answer, they can become confusing. It needs a very clear head and complete concentration to read all the alternative answers, and also a really careful reading of each question to determine exactly what is being asked.

Here are the answers to the 11 questions, and in the case of multiple choice questions, these are the only correct answers.

1   E

This answer can be arrived at by a process of elimination. **A** is obviously put in for those who are politically left-wing and who equate Western civilization with capitalism. This is where preconceived ideas could cloud your response to what the author is saying. His is not a political argument. **B** is put in for the careless reader for whom the word *Western* means a cowboy film. This seems a silly alternative for the careful reader; but some candidates do read so superficially that Western = American film about the Wild West, and therefore they put down **B**. At first glance **C** seems a possible answer; but, on more careful consideration you should realize it is not correct because there are many districts in the world which could by no stretch of imagination be called 'contemporary Western civilization' yet where primitive life has been wiped out by modern progress (Africa, China, India etc.). So, as a definition, this alternative is too wide and inaccurate. **D** is put in for the confused reader who hasn't clearly followed the argument of the passage, but thinks it must be something rather bookish and upper-class. This leaves **E** as the only possible answer, and although the phrase 'contemporary Western civilization' is sometimes used loosely to include such countries as Australia and New Zealand, 'typical districts of modern Europe and America' is the best explanation for the expression.

2   A

In this question the important words are *as used in lines 10–11*. The more usual meaning of 'abscond' is 'escape from authority'; but that is not what it means here, so **B** is not correct. The word 'abscond' is often also associated with 'avoiding lawful arrest', but if you substitute these words in the sentence, they do not have the same meaning as the original word, so **C** is also wrong. The burglar could possibly, later on, 'hide away temporarily' the property he has taken, or could 'make a profit' from it, but he cannot do that until after he has 'absconded' with it, so **D** and **E** are not correct. That leaves **A** as the only correct answer, and if you put 'go away secretly' into the sentence in place of the word 'abscond', you will find you retain the same meaning.

3   E

This is a question where you must retain the drift of the whole paragraph in your mind. **A, B, C,** and **D** all include individual factors that are mentioned somewhere in the paragraph – 'food', 'burglary', 'war', 'fighting' – but none of these sums up the argument of the whole of the paragraph as well as E – 'resentment against intruders'. In fact, a good summary of the first paragraph would be: The most obvious mark of the territorial animal is its resentment against intruders.

---

4 B

The chief difficulty here is the word *accommodate*. The more usual sense is to find a house, or place to live; so, to a careless reader, A, D or E seem possible. But that is not what *accommodate* means in this passage. If you had read the passage carefully enough, you would have realized that here the word is used in its alternative sense of to 'adapt', or 'adjust', making B or C possible. The choice between these two is difficult; but a careful reading of the sentence reveals that the author is here talking about our 'natural attitudes' rather than our 'everyday needs', so B is the best answer.

---

5 C

This question is best answered by checking the alternatives against the phrase 'an inevitable sequel of urbanization' as it is used in the sentence in the passage, and finding one which will fit into this sentence without changing the meaning. There are three words for which you must find equivalents: 'inevitable', 'sequel', and 'urbanization'; C is the only alternative which has a suitable combination to fit all three.

---

6 D

A, B, and C cancel themselves out, because there is no evidence in the sentence that people 'keep away from others' or 'behave aggressively'; neither is there evidence in the sentence in lines 19–22 about 'open rural spaces'. Which leaves D or E. But E overstates the case because there is no evidence that people are forced to 'check all' their inner 'feelings', only their 'aggressive impulses'. So that leaves D, which does give the reason why 'people find life in cities irritating and exhausting'.

---

7 D

This question is just about a repeat of question 6; but this time all the other alternatives are so obviously wrong, that D is the only possible answer, if you have understood the writer's argument.

8   C

This is another question which is best answered by a process of elimination. **A** is not correct because it obviously overstates the case. **B** is incorrect because the example of country life is brought in only as a contrast, and not as the main content of the paragraph. The 'inevitability of urbanization' is not discussed at all in this paragraph, so **E** is wrong. This leaves us with **C** or **D**. **D** is, however, too vague a summary because the paragraph does not discuss primitive impulses in general, but only those associated with overcrowding. Furthermore, the paragraph doesn't say that city dwellers 'learn how to control their primitive impulses'. This leaves us with **C**, which, once again, is a good summary of the whole paragraph.

9   D

This is a difficult question because you first of all have to decide what *is* the author's main argument: it could be summarized thus: Man is a territorial animal, and, as such, dislikes his territory being invaded. We now have to find *the best evidence* to support this argument. When you have sorted this out, you soon realize that **A**, **B**, **C** and **E** offer no evidence to support this argument. **D** is, in fact, the only alternative that does.

10   D

This is another question where your own preconceived ideas could cause you to give the wrong answer; it is quite likely that you have your own ideas on why man can be regarded as an animal; but the answer we want is the chief reason given in the passage. **D** is the only possible answer.

11   B

Here you are asked to hold in your mind the purpose of the whole passage, and not separate sentences in it. You could find parts of the passage which seem to suggest **A**, **C**, or **D**, but they are only given as *examples* for the main purpose of the whole passage, which is to explain some of the behaviour of city dwellers.

To summarize the points made on the answers to this passage:

1 It is necessary in comprehension to understand not only the individual parts of the passage, but the main drift and argument of the whole passage.

2 If the passage is on a topic on which you have ideas of your own, you must not let them cloud your appreciation of what the writer is saying; your own views are not wanted here, and can be a hindrance if you are not prepared to keep an open mind.

3 You must not only read the passage carefully, but also read each question carefully, to make sure you answer exactly what you are asked to answer. And with multiple choice questions, you must also read every alternative carefully. The correct answer is often not as obvious as it first appears.

4 Multiple choice questions need a clear head and complete concentration, because the alternatives are usually very close to being correct answers.

5 Watch out for words which are used in an unusual sense; they can mislead you into an inaccurate reading, and you can be sure that any words which are used in an unusual way will probably occur in the questions.

6 Make sure you keep a versatility of response to the questions and the alternatives. The questions often switch from those on the meaning of individual words, or of individual sentences, or of the paragraphs, or of the whole passage. Or some can ask for evidence, or examples. You must quickly switch your response to see that one question is quite different from the last.

7 Timing is particularly important in all questions, but especially so in multiple choice questions. In the paper from which the passage in this chapter was taken, there were altogether three passages, totalling about 2500 words (that is about 5 pages of this book) and 60 multiple choice questions which had to be answered within $1\frac{1}{4}$ hours. At first glance, this looks a formidable amount, and many candidates are tempted to start on the questions straightaway, and not read the passages carefully. This, however, is a great mistake. As we have seen, most of the questions cannot be answered unless you have thoroughly understood the meaning, tone and intention of each passage, and this can only be achieved after two readings. Then, if you do know what the passages are about, most multiple choice questions can be answered in a matter of seconds, rather than minutes, because there is no writing to do. So a rough guide could be 40 minutes to answer 60 questions, 5 minutes to check over, which leaves 30 minutes for reading the three passages.

8 Full instructions for answering multiple choice questions are always given on the question paper. (The time to read these instructions is

not included in the time allowed to answer the questions.) Usually, you are given an answer sheet which is numbered for the number of questions in your test, and against each number you have four or five letters, A to D, or A to E. You then have to shade over the letter which you think gives the correct answer. The answer sheet is then fed into a machine which records the correct answers. That's why everything on your answer sheet must be neat, clean, tidy and exact. The machine will not differentiate between careless, unintentional marks, and your intended answers.

Examination practice

1 Read carefully the following passage, and answer the questions set on it.
(ox)

In general usage, the word *history* has, and has had, several meanings which need to be carefully unravelled. Like its European equivalents, it is based on a Greek word meaning 'knowledge' or 'inquiry'. Perhaps the English phrase which comes closest to the
5   Greek is *Natural History*, which is an inquiry into the world of plants and animals. But because any form of knowledge or inquiry is bound to take notice of the element of time, and particularly of time past, history became increasingly associated with the past, and the changes which time has brought. Darwin's theory of
10   evolution is a classic demonstration of this in the study of the natural order. In fact several scientific specializations like geology, palaeontology and astronomy are as concerned with time as is the orthodox historian in the field of purely human affairs.

Gradually two broad meanings of the word *history* emerged. The
15   first was a relation of events, a narrative or story – whether true or imaginary. When in the 18th century the English novelist Henry Fielding wrote his characterful 'histories' (of Tom Jones, Jonathan Wild, Joseph Andrews, etc.) he was using the word as simply a story, and this still remains of course one meaning of the modern
20   French *histoire*. The second, narrower meaning is the narrative or record of the human past, which is, professedly at least, true. This covers the constructed account of past events by the historian, and is of course the normal use of the word in English today. In this sense history obviously includes the work of both historians and
25   archaeologists, as they both contribute to the record of human life in the past (regardless of the fact that they use different kinds of evidence).

More recently another quite specialized meaning has come into circulation, though it is rarely found in dictionaries. It denotes the
30 study of the human past *from documentary sources alone*. By documents, we mean all written sources, whether manuscript, printed or inscribed. This is primarily of course the field of the regular historian, whose job it is to interpret written or verbal evidence.

This last meaning of the word is used by archaeologists when they
35 refer to prehistory, proto-history and the like. Here *history* means the written records of literate societies, referring to themselves and sometimes their illiterate neighbours. Before the advent of literacy (or its survival), the human past can only be studied from physical or archaeological traces. By *prehistoric* some archaeologists mean
40 societies which existed before there was documentary evidence anywhere, that is before approximately 3000 BC when written records first appear in the Near East. Others, not so ruthlessly logical, call societies prehistoric which pre-date the *local* arrival of literacy. In spite of this difference of opinion, all are agreed that
45 *history* in this connection means written records. It is of some interest that the coining of the term *prehistoric* in the 19th century seems to have fostered the narrow definition of *history*. In other words, people with largely archaeological interests encouraged, and perhaps even originated, a new definition of the word *history*,
50 because they wished to emphasize the crucial difference between periods that are documented and those that are not.

D. P. DYMOND, *Archaeology and History* (Thames and Hudson).

(a) *The author tells us that our word* history *is based on a Greek word meaning* knowledge *or* inquiry.
   (i) *What English phrase does he quote that exemplifies this original meaning?*
   (ii) *What do you understand by* its European equivalents *(lines 2–3)?*
   (4 marks)
(b) *Since its appearance in English the word* history *has acquired a number of different meanings. In a paragraph of some 80–100 words trace these developments.*   (20 marks)
(c) *Of the different meanings, which one is no longer in common use in English?*   (4 marks)
(d) (i) *Give the meanings as here used, of the words* literate *and* illiterate *(lines 36–7).*
   (ii) The local arrival of literacy *(lines 43–4). Explain 'local'.*
   (6 marks)

    (e) *What do you understand by people* with largely archaeological
    interests (*line 48*)?   (6 marks)

2 *The following passage was written by a reporter from England describing*
  a visit to America twenty years ago. Read it carefully, and then answer
  the questions that follow.   (JMB)

    The West is the land of the adventurer; not only the cowboy,
and the Indian scout, but also the prospector – and the presence of
the miner still contributes to the flavour of the place. All over the
uranium regions you can see little one-horse uranium mines – a
5 shaft-head and a hut or two, just like the shattered shanties that
stand in Nevada as memorials to the gold bonanzas. For such
operators, undaunted by the hideous legends of Hiroshima, there
are profitable if disconcerting sidelines. 'When the human body is
exposed to a bombardment of gamma rays, many of these rays pass
10 completely through the body without any effect, but many collide
with electrons of various cells of the body, knocking the electrons
away from their atoms, thus ionizing those cells.' So says a pseudo-
scientific brochure issued by one of the many uranium mines
which invite sufferers from rheumatism and other afflictions to sit
15 in their underground tunnels and be bombarded.
    'Miraculous' cures are reported. One mine claims that a crippled
English sheepdog was totally restored to health. Many others
publish grateful letters claiming instant cures, amazing reliefs,
improvements when all hope had been abandoned, shattering
20 experiences on the train home.
    There is something about all this that brings the wanderer very
near the heyday of the West, when prospectors made their fortunes
overnight in lonely gulches or squalid mining camps. At Deadwood,
South Dakota (the home of Deadwood Dick, the Deadwood Gulch,
25 the Deadwood Stage, Wild Bill Hickock and Calamity Jane), I talked
to an elderly woman in a shop about the town's famous days –
when the prospectors were greedily working all down the gulch;
when the stage left each week with its cargo of gold for the perilous
journey to Denver, through Buffalo Gap, Red Canyon, past the
30 threatening haunts of Peg-legged Bradley, Curley Grimes and
other ruthless buccaneers of that legendary road. 'How long ago
it seems,' I said with a sigh, looking around me at the counters full
of Colgate's and home permanents. 'It might almost be another

world.' The woman seemed a trifle put out. 'Well, I don't know,'
35 she said testily. 'I don't remember Wild Bill Hickock, but I
remember Potato Creek Johnny well enough, and you wouldn't
call me an old woman, would you, or perhaps you would?' So
saying, she opened her handbag and produced a snapshot. It was
of old Johnny himself, one of the best-remembered of the Dead-
40 wood prospectors, who made strike after strike, but never acquired
a fortune. There he was, staring at me from the picture with bright,
bird-like eyes, his face enshrouded in a vast tangled beard, on his
head a crumpled black hat, his old shirt open at the neck, in his hand
a large gold nugget, a symbol of his fluctuating fortune. 'He was as
45 nice an old fellow as you could meet,' said the woman, replacing
the photograph in her handbag with (I thought) the faint suspicion
of a snuffle, 'so don't you go saying he was like something from
another world.'
 She was perfectly right. Those beloved adventurers lived in the
50 recent past, and the rumbustious tradition of the American frontier
was established in our grandfathers' time. I made a pilgrimage to
Wild Bill Hickock's grave, on the side of a hill outside Deadwood,
and found it decent and well cared-for. Hickock, who was Marshal
of the town, was murdered in a Deadwood tavern with a revolver
55 shot in the back. This is his second burial place. In Deadwood I
came across the memoirs of one of the undertaker's men who had
helped to move the body to the cemetery on the hill. He first gave
some agreeably horrific glimpses of life for an undertaker in the
great days of Deadwood, when bodies were lying about all over the
60 place, in smoky taverns, or in lonely thickets, and then he described
the reburial of Wild Bill. 'When we dug up Wild Bill,' he wrote,
'he still looked natural as life. Only his hair and whiskers had grown.
But the air done something to the corpse. The air made Bill sink in,
crumble, or something. We buried him up on the mountain.'

(a) *What similarities does the author suggest, in the first paragraph,
 between the gold-mining carried on in the West in the past and the
 uranium-mining carried on in the present? What were the
 similarities in the approach of the miners to their work?* (5 marks)
(b) *The author seems very doubtful about the effectiveness of the use of
 gamma rays in the uranium mines as a treatment for disease.
 Beginning a new line for each, write down four of the author's
 phrases in the first two paragraphs (lines 6–20) which seem to you*

to indicate his doubts, and in each case justify your choice with a
brief comment.   (8 marks)

(c) (i) Basing your answer on the evidence of lines 21–34, suggest in
your own words what can be learned about the activities and
characteristics of the prospectors and of the buccaneers, in
'the heyday of the West'.   (10 marks)

(ii) What does the photograph of Potato Creek Johnny suggest
about the sort of person he was? Justify each point you make
by a brief quotation from the passage.   (8 marks)

(d) (i) Explain why the author's remark, 'How long ago it seems',
(lines 31–2), was made when he was in the shop.

(ii) Why was the woman in the shop 'a trifle put out' (line 34)?

(iii) What does the author imply about the reason for the elderly
woman's feelings when he mentions 'the faint suspicion of a
snuffle' (lines 46–7)?   (6 marks)

(e) The last paragraph describes a visit made by the author to Wild
Bill Hickock's grave.

(i) Quote the word which suggests that the author's reason for
visiting Hickock's grave was more than casual interest.

(ii) What does the state of the grave imply about the attitude of
the people of Deadwood to Hickock?

(iii) Why do you think the author uses the word 'agreeably' in
referring to the 'horrific glimpses of life for an undertaker in
the great days of Deadwood' (lines 58–9)?

(iv) How does the quotation from the undertaker's memoirs (lines
61–4) suggest that he was not a well-educated man?   (7 marks)

(f) In one word or one short phrase only, explain the meaning of each
of the following words as used in the passage:
(i) undaunted (line 7); (ii) heyday (line 22); (iii) legendary (line 31);
(iv) testily (line 35); (v) fluctuating (line 44); (vi) thickets (line 60).
(6 marks)

(g) What does the list of names (lines 23–5) suggest about the reasons
for the author's visit to Deadwood?   (2 marks)   (JMB)

3 Read the following passage carefully, then read the directions after it.
(LOND)

In those days when I was a little girl, there were bitter winters
and burning summers. Since then I have known summers which,
when I close my eyes, are the colour of ochre-yellow earth,
cracking between stalks of corn. But no summer, save those of

5   my childhood, enshrines the memory of scarlet geraniums and the
glowing spikes of foxgloves. No winter now is ever pure white
beneath a sky charged with slate-coloured clouds foretelling a
storm of thicker snowflakes yet to come, and thereafter a thaw
glittering with a thousand waterdrops and bright with spear-
10   shaped buds. How the sky used to lour over the snow-laden roof
of the haylofts, the weathercock, and the bare boughs of the walnut
tree, making the she-cats flatten their ears! The quiet vertical fall
of the snow became oblique and, as I wandered about the garden
catching its flying flakes in my mouth, a faint booming as of a
15   distant sea arose above my hooded head. My mother would come
out on the terrace, sample the weather, and call out to me:

'A gale from the west! Run and shut the skylights in the barn!
And the door of the coach house! And the window of the back
room!'

20   Eager cabin boy of the family vessel, I would rush off, my clogs
clattering, thrilled if, from the depths of this hissing turmoil of
white and blue-black, a flash of lightning and a brief mutter of
thunder together filled one of the abysses of the sky. I would try
then to shudder and believe that the end of the world had come.

25   But when the din was at its height, there would be my mother,
peering through a big brass-rimmed magnifying glass, lost in
wonder as she counted the branched crystals of a handful of snow
she had just snatched from the very jaws of the West Wind as it
flung itself upon our garden.

Directions

*Each question has five suggested answers. Select the best answer to
each question and write down the letter accordingly.* (LOND)

1 *The she-cats 'flattened their
ears' (line 12) because they*

A *were covered with snow*

B *felt overcome with the cold*

C *were ruffled by the wind*

D *felt a menace in the weather*

E *were soaked in water-drops*

2 *Which one of the following
is closest in meaning to
'oblique' as used in line 13?*

A *slanting*

B *heavy*

C *parallel*

D *audible*

E *swirling*

3 *The 'faint booming', referred to
in line 14, was probably the
distant sound of*

A *high winds*

B *the sea*

C *storm signals*

D *the thunder*

E slamming doors

4 The statement that the mother would 'sample the weather' (line 16) is best explained as meaning she would

A take a handful of snow

B test the temperature in the garden

C form a quick impression of the conditions

D decide what immediate steps must be taken

E forecast the coming of the storm

5 The coming of the storm was heralded by all of the following EXCEPT the

A appearance of the clouds

B aspect of the sky

C behaviour of the cats

D sound of the waves

E direction of the wind

6 The author thought of herself as the 'eager cabin boy of the family vessel' (line 20) for all the following reasons EXCEPT that she

A was keen to carry out the orders given

B enjoyed the sense of serving in a post of danger

C performed all her duties without understanding why

D believed that she was helping to protect her home

E accepted her position as the junior member of the family

7 The mother's reaction to 'the din' (line 25) was one of

A alarm

B unconcern

C bewilderment

D defiance

E wonder

8 Which one of the following is closest in meaning to 'peering' as used in line 26?

A glaring

B staring open-eyed

C peeping

D looking intently

E gazing

9 The mother's behaviour before and during the storm (lines 15–29) could properly be described as all the following EXCEPT

A investigating

B frightened

C decisive

D fascinated

E foreseeing

10 The author's mood as she recalls her childhood is best described as one of

A ecstasy

B amazement

C melancholy

D nostalgia

E anxiety

11 All the following contrasts are made in the passage EXCEPT

A land and sea noises

B light and darkness

C stillness and commotion

D past and present

E sombre and vivid colours

5 Grammar

Few boards set separate questions on grammar, but all boards often refer to grammatical terms within the wording of questions, such words as *noun, phrase, subject, preposition* etc. So even if the syllabus of your board does not include questions on grammar, it is as well that you do know some grammatical terms. You can then be sure you are doing the correct thing when a question asks you to name a phrase, or noun, or preposition.

This chapter is not a complete manual of English grammar, but it does contain everything you need to know for the English Language examination, even for those boards which do set questions on grammar. This chapter is also useful for some of the questions, set by several boards, where you are asked to correct errors in sentences. Some of these errors are grammatical, and it is difficult to deal with such questions if you have no knowledge of grammar. This knowledge could also be useful in helping you to correct some of your own errors.

Grammar is an attempt to explain how a language works. Different languages need different grammars, because not all languages work in the same way. In a tonal language, Yoruba for example, the meaning of words depends on whether the voice goes up or down when different syllables are spoken; the grammar of written Yoruba therefore includes a system of marks written or printed above or below different letters. Written English, fortunately, is not quite so complicated, and because the grammar of written English approximates to Latin, the terms used to describe how Latin works are also used for English.

When attempting to describe how anything works, a car engine for example, it is best to start by learning the names of the individual parts. It is then possible to explain how the parts are put together. The smallest individual units that need concern us here are words. So we will begin by learning the names of the different kinds of words used in the English Language. There are eight, which are usually known as the parts of speech.

Parts of speech

1 *Noun:* a word used for naming a thing.
2 *Pronoun:* a word used in place of a noun.
3 *Adjective:* a word which qualifies a noun.
4 *Verb:* a word which denotes actions, states or happenings.
5 *Adverb:* a word which qualifies a verb, adjective, or another adverb.
6 *Preposition:* a word which shows in what relation one thing stands to another.
7 *Conjunction:* a word used to connect one part of a sentence with another.
8 *Interjection:* a word which has no grammatical connection with the sentence.

Examples of parts of speech

Nouns   There are five kinds of nouns:
1 *Common* – the names of all physical objects:
    cow, tree, girl, desk.
2 *Proper* – the names of people, towns, countries etc., which are always spelt with a capital letter:
    James, Manchester, February, Monday, France.
3 *Abstract* – the names of non-physical things:
    freedom, poverty, pride.
4 *Collective* – the names of collections of things:
    flock, team, regiment.
5 *Material* – the names of materials:
    water, metal, plastic, nylon.

Pronouns   There are four kinds of pronouns:
1 *Personal,* which have the following forms –
    (a) Nominative: i.e. subject of a verb:
        I, we, he, you, they.
    (b) Objective: i.e. object of a verb or preposition:
        me, us, him, you, them.
    (c) Possessive: i.e. denoting possession:
        mine, ours, his, yours, theirs.

(d) Reflexive: refers back to (or reflects) a previous noun or pronoun:
myself, ourselves, himself, themselves.

2 *Demonstrative* – words which are substituted for the noun to which
they refer:
this, that, these, those.

NB When these words are used with a noun they become
demonstrative adjectives:

(i) I like *that*: '*that*' = demonstrative pronoun.

(ii) I like *that* cake: '*that*' = demonstrative adjective.

3 *Relative* – words which relate a clause to a previous noun, which is
called the antecedent:
who, which, whose, whom, that.

NB These are sometimes called conjunctive pronouns, because they
connect the clause they introduce with the rest of the sentence:
This is the road *which* I mean.

4 *Interrogative* – pronouns which introduce a question:
who, which, whose, whom, what, when used as in:
Who is that?

Adjectives There are nine kinds of adjectives:

1 *Descriptive* – gives some descriptive detail of a noun:
He saw a *wild* cat.

2 *Proper* – formed from proper nouns, and, like them, have capital
letters:
They have an *Italian* cook.

3 *Possessive* – words denoting possession of the noun:
The cat hurt *its* tail.

4 *Numerical* – numbers, either cardinal or ordinal, used with nouns:
I have *three* books.

5 *Indefinite* – words which denote quantity, but give no exact
information:
All boys should go.

6 *Demonstrative* – the words *this, that, these, those,* when used with
nouns:
I like *that* house.

7 *Interrogative* – words such as *which* and *what*, used with nouns to
introduce a question:
Which tree do you mean?

8 *Distributive* – the words *each, every, either, neither,* when used with
nouns:

He went *every* day.

9 *Comparative* – the words *less, least, more, most,* when qualifying nouns:

He made the *least* effort.

NB   The indefinite article *a* and the definite article *the* are usually classified as adjectives.

Most adjectives can be used in two ways:

(a) Attributively: i.e. qualifying the noun directly, usually placed before it:

There goes the *black* dog.

(b) As a predicate: i.e. a verb comes between the noun and its adjective:

The dog was *black.*

Verbs   There are three kinds of verbs:

1 *Transitive* – a verb whose sense demands an object:

He *hit* the dog.

(If you *hit*, you must hit something, and that something is the object.)

2 *Intransitive* – a verb which cannot have an object because the action affects only the subject:

He *laughed.*

NB   There are some intransitive verbs which do not take an object, but whose sense needs completing. The verb *to be* is the most common:

He *is* king.

You cannot *is* anything, so *king* is not the object. It is called the *complement.*

3 *Auxiliary* – a verb used to help form a tense or mood of another verb:

He *had* laughed.

Tense   The main tenses in English verbs are past, present and future. They can be subdivided as follows:

	Past	*Present*	*Future*
Indefinite	I sang	I sing	I shall sing
Continuous	I was singing	I am singing	I shall be singing
Perfect	I had sung	I have sung	I shall have sung
Cont. Perfect	I had been singing	I have been singing	I shall have been singing

Active and Passive   A verb is *active* when the subject is doing the action. A verb is *passive* when someone or something other than the subject is doing the action:

Active: The boy *gave* a book to the girl.
Passive: The girl *was given* a book by the boy.
 or A book *was given* to the girl by the boy.

Mood There are four moods of the verb in English:
1 *Infinitive* – the form of the verb which is not limited by number or person. It can be past or present:
 Past: *to have done.*
 Present: *to do.*
2 *Indicative* – this makes an assertion, or inquiry, or states a fact:
 He *did* this. *Did* you do this?
3 *Imperative* – this gives a command or advice:
 Do this.
NB The subject, *you*, is understood.
4 *Subjunctive* – this expresses a supposition, wish or order, likelihood or hypothesis, i.e. not a definite fact:
 If I *were* king.
NB The indicative, imperative and subjunctive moods are always finite, that is they must have a subject with which they must agree; a singular noun must have a singular verb etc.

Participles These are used in two ways:
1 adjectivally in phrases:
 Jane, *being* good at hockey, was chosen.
2 with auxiliary verbs to form tenses:
 She is *going*.
 Participles have the following forms:

	Active	*Passive*
Present	teaching	being taught
Perfect	having taught	having been taught
Past		taught

The gerund This is the '-ing' form of a verb, but used as a noun:
His *speaking* came as a surprise.

Adverbs These can qualify verbs, adjectives, or other adverbs:
Verb . . . . He spoke *quickly*.
Adjective . . . . He was *very* old.
Adverb . . . . He spoke *really* well.
There are two types of adverbs:
1 *Simple* – these say *how, why, when, where,* or *how often*;

affirm or *deny*; or, when used with an adjective or adverb, say *how much*:

>He went *there*.
>
>He *certainly* did speak.
>
>She played *rather* badly.

2 *Interrogative* – used to introduce questions:

>*How* do you do this?

NB An adverb is sometimes used as a complement:

>They were *out*.

This is called the predicative use of the adverb.

Prepositions Grammatically, a preposition must always be followed by a noun or its equivalent, which it is said to govern. It is sometimes called the object of the preposition because the noun or pronoun must be in the objective case:

>We received the message *from* them.

In colloquial speech the preposition sometimes comes after the word it governs:

>Whom did you hear that *from*?

The pronoun *whom* is in the objective case because it is governed by the preposition *from*.

NB A preposition is sometimes followed by an adverb:

>Try to be ready *by then*.

When the object of a preposition is omitted, the preposition becomes an adverb:

>I saw her *outside* the house.
>
>I saw her *outside*.

Conjunctions There are two kinds of conjunctions:

1 *Co-ordinative* – those that join words, phrases, clauses or sentences of equal importance:

>Jim *and* Tom went.
>
>Go away *but* come back soon.

2 *Subordinative* – those that link a subordinative clause or phrase to the rest of the sentence:

>He asked me *how* I did it.

Interjections Words, usually exclamations, which have no grammatical connection with the sentence, and can be removed without altering the sense:

>*Well*, that was not what I expected.

Concluding note on the parts of speech

You determine the part of speech of each word by its function in the sentence. The same word can have several different jobs, and is therefore a different part of speech on each occasion:

I like *that*	:	*that* =	pronoun.
I like *that* cake	:	*that* =	adjective.
I don't like it *that* much	:	*that* =	adverb.
He said *that* he didn't know	:	*that* =	conjunction.

The sentence

The basis of every sentence is a finite verb, and as a finite verb must have a subject, the shortest sentence must have two words:

Subject   Verb
Jesus   wept.

A sentence which has only one finite verb is called a *simple sentence*.

If the verb is transitive (i.e. one which demands an object) we must have at least three words:

Subject Verb Object
Boys tell   stories.

All the words which are not part of the subject are called the *predicate*.

From this basic structure, sentences of any length can be built up. We can add an indirect object, and extend the subject and object by adding adjectives, and the verb by adding an adverb:

Subject   Predicate
Little boys often tell me tall stories.

NB   The indirect object always has *to* or *from* understood.

Phrases

A phrase is a group of words – but without a finite verb – which does the same work in a sentence as an adjective, adverb or noun. So we can extend the sentence by adding phrases:

Subject   Predicate

Boys fond of fishing   tell, on arriving home, stories with happy endings.

The sentence remains a simple sentence because it still has only one finite verb.

Examples of the three kinds of phrases

Adjectival   They do the same work as adjectives:

Boys tell stories *with happy endings*.

Adverbial   There are eight kinds which do the same work as adverbs:
1 *Reason (or cause)*: She shouted *to attract attention*.
2 *Purpose*: He worked *to have a chance of passing*.
3 *Condition*: *Weather permitting*, play will start soon.
4 *Manner*: She sang *like a skylark*.
5 *Time*: He arrived *at noon*.
6 *Concession*: *While allowing that point*, I still disagree.
7 *Place*: He came *from London*.

Noun   There are five kinds of noun phrases:
1 *Subject*: *Helping to cook* is her hobby.
2 *Object*: She likes *to help the cook*.
3 *Complement*: He is *acting as referee*.
4 *in apposition*: Beethoven, *composer of the Choral Symphony*, was deaf.
5 *Governed by a preposition*: He gained nothing by *going abroad*.

Clauses

A clause is a part of a sentence which contains a finite verb and does the same work as a noun, adjective or adverb. (A finite verb is a verb which has a subject with which it agrees.) So we could extend our sentence by adding one or more subordinate clauses:

      Subject   *Predicate*
Boys who like fishing   tell stories which have happy endings.
The sentence then becomes a *complex sentence*, i.e. one which contains one main clause, and one or more subordinate clauses.

Examples of the four kinds of clauses

There are four kinds of clauses, Main, Adjectival, Adverbial and Noun:

Main clause   The basis of every sentence: as every tree must have a trunk, every sentence must have a main clause. The part of the sentence which is *not* in italics in all the examples below is the main clause:
This sentence has a main clause *which has six words*.

Adjectival clause   This describes a noun:
    I shot the dog *which worried the sheep*.
You should write this out like this:
    I shot the dog = main clause.
    which worried the sheep = adjectival clause describing 'dog'.
NB   This is the house *where I live*.
    where I live = adjectival clause describing 'house'.

This is the hour *when owls cry*.
when owls cry = adjectival clause describing 'hour'.

Adverbial clauses   These modify a verb or adjective. There are nine kinds.
1 *Result*: He was *so* fat *that he stuck in the door.*
2 *Cause*: I hit him *because he was cheeky.*
3 *Purpose*: He trained *so that he might win.*
4 *Condition*: You will fail *if you are idle.*
5 *Manner*: She ran *as if she had a lion chasing her.*
6 *Time*: Go *when I tell you.*
7 *Concession*: *Although he is young* he is wise.
8 *Comparison*: He is not *as* old *as I thought.*
9 *Place*: Go *where I tell you.*

Noun clauses   These take the place of nouns in sentences. There are five kinds.
1 *Subject of verb*: *What you said* is true.
2 *Object of verb*: I think *that you will pass.*
3 *Complement of verb*: The result was *what I expected.*
4 *In apposition to another noun*: He gave an order *that all the boys were to wear ties.*
5 *Governed by a preposition*: I am learning nothing from *what I am doing.*

With the information given above, it is possible to answer correctly a question on grammar such as the following, set in the English Intermediate Certificate Examination by the Irish Board (An Roinn Oidea-chais):

The pudding had been <u>completely</u> burned when the cook took <u>it from the oven</u>.
(*a*) *Write out separately the clauses in the sentence.*
(*b*) *Say what kind the subordinate clause is and what its function is.*
(*c*) *Write out separately the subject and predicate of the principal clause.*
(*d*) *Say what part of speech each of the underlined words is.*   (ARO)

These questions should be answered as follows:

(a) When asked to write out the separate clauses in a sentence, the first thing to decide is how many clauses there are. Each clause has a finite verb. (A finite verb has a subject.) Therefore the first thing to do is to find your finite verbs.

In the last example there are two finite verbs:

had been burned – subject = *the pudding*

took – subject = *the cook*

There are therefore two clauses, which should be written out as follows:

(a) (i) The pudding had been completely burned

  (ii) when the cook took it from the oven

(b) The principal (or main) clause of this sentence is *The pudding had been completely burned*. Therefore the other clause written out in (a) above is the subordinate clause. To answer the questions *what kind the subordinate clause is* and *what its function is*, you need to ask yourself what it is doing in the sentence. Which word is it modifying?

The answer is *burned*, which is a verb. Therefore the clause must be an adverbial clause.

Then you must decide *how* it is modifying the verb. There are nine different ways that an adverbial clause can modify a verb. (Turn back to p 119 and look them up.)

This clause is telling you *when* the pudding was *burned*. It is therefore an adverbial clause of time.

This should be written out as follows:

(b) adverbial clause of time modifying 'burned'.

(c) Here you are asked to write out the *subject* and *predicate* of the principal clause, and not of the whole sentence. The principal clause is:

The pudding had been completely burned.

On p 117 you learned that *all the words which are not part of the subject are called the predicate*.

In this clause the verb is *had been burned* and the thing that had been burned was *the pudding*. The question should therefore be answered as follows:

(c) subject = the pudding

  predicate = had been completely burned

(d) To determine the parts of speech of the two words *completely* and *from*, you must ask yourself what the function of each is in the sentence.

Completely is telling you how the pudding had been burned. *Had been burned* is a verb. Because it is qualifying a verb, *completely* must therefore be an adverb.

From is governing the noun phrase *the oven*. It is showing where the pudding was in relationship to the oven. It is therefore a preposition.

The answer should be written out as follows:

(d) completely = adverb; from = preposition

When writing out answers to questions such as these, make sure that what you intend is perfectly clear. Leave plenty of space, and number each answer carefully. It is up to you to make the answer clear to the examiner; he has no time to sort out what you intended.

Examination practice

1 *Write out the following sentences, one word under the other, down the left-hand side of the page. Then name the parts of speech of each word and give its grammatical function in the sentence:*
   (a) There was a rush of the sea into the cave, which carried there large, drifting masses of seaweed, leaving them among the rocks when the tide went out.
   (b) When she was told that the cove, and the sea running into it, were not the property of her grandfather she understood that the statement might be true.
   (c) As she looked at him, in that instant, she could see that his eyes were open and that he was struggling with his hands.
2 *Write out: (i) all the adjectival phrases; (ii) all the adverbial phrases; (iii) all the noun phrases from the sentences in Question 1, and say what each is doing in the sentence in which it appears.*
3 *Write out separately all the clauses in the three sentences in Question 1. Give the grammatical name and function of each clause.*
4 *Write a sentence which contains a noun clause, an adverbial clause and an adjectival clause. Then write out each clause separately, and say what it is doing in the sentence.*
5 *In the following sentences, substitute clauses for the words underlined:*
   (a) The old woman died. (b) I shall go without your permission.
   (c) The question was too difficult to answer. (d) Their story is true.
   (e) We could not hear his words. (f) His reply was lost.

6 Direct and Indirect Speech

Several boards sometimes set a question on direct and indirect speech. The Associated Examining Board, for example, says: 'Questions may also be set on English usage: for example, direct and indirect speech, the correct use of parts of speech' (which was dealt with in the last chapter), 'and idiomatic and metaphorical expressions' (which will be covered in the next chapter).

Direct speech is used when the words written down are the actual words spoken by some person, or are words written as a personal statement of some kind, such as an autobiography.

Indirect (or 'reported') speech is used when a person reports direct speech, that is he writes the words in the past tense and refers to the original speakers or writers in the third person. But, as far as possible, the same words and tone should be kept. For example, if the original direct speech is old-fashioned, when it is transposed into indirect speech, it should still have an old-fashioned flavour, and not be modernized. That is paraphrase, which is discussed in Chapter 8 of this book.

In the following examples each passage is given first as direct speech, and then as indirect speech.

1 Direct speech
'Biddy,' said I with some severity, 'I have particular reasons for wanting to be a gentleman.'

'You know best, Pip; but don't you think you are happier as you are?'

'Biddy,' I exclaimed impatiently, 'I am not at all happy as I am. I am disgusted with my life.'

From *Great Expectations* by Dickens.

Indirect speech
Pip said, with some severity, that he had particular reasons for wanting to be a gentleman. Biddy replied that he knew best, but wondered if he

didn't think he was happier as he was. Pip exclaimed impatiently that he was not at all happy as he was. He was disgusted with his life.

Notes:

(a) Inverted commas are not used.

(b) There is no new paragraph for each speaker.

(c) All pronouns are in the third person.

(d) All verbs are in the past tense.

(e) The word 'wondered' is inserted to give the tone of the original piece.

2 Direct speech

'When I find myself growing grim about the mouth; whenever it is a damp, drizzly November in my soul; whenever I find myself involuntarily pausing before coffin warehouses, and bringing up the rear of every funeral I meet – then I account it high time to get to sea as soon as I can. This is my substitute for pistol and ball.'

Ishmael, the hero of *Moby Dick*, is telling his story.

Indirect speech

Ishmael, the hero of *Moby Dick*, said that whenever he found himself growing grim about the mouth; whenever it was a damp, drizzly November in his soul; whenever he found himself involuntarily pausing before coffin warehouses, and bringing up the rear of every funeral he met – then he accounted it high time to get to sea as soon as he could. That was his substitute for pistol and ball.

Notes:

(a) The introductory 'Ishmael, the hero of *Moby Dick*, said that . . .' is used to explain who is speaking.

(b) 'This' in the last sentence of the original becomes 'that' in indirect speech. Similarly 'these' becomes 'those', 'here' becomes 'there', etc.

3 Direct speech in a play

Marlow: What a tedious uncomfortable day we have had of it! We were told it was but forty miles and we have come above threescore!

Hastings (flinging himself down into a chair): And all, Marlow, from that unaccountable reserve of yours that would not let us inquire more frequently on the way.

Marlow: I own, Hastings, I am unwilling to lay myself under an obligation to everyone I meet.

Hastings: At present, however, we are not likely to receive any answer.

From *She Stoops to Conquer*, by Goldsmith.

Indirect speech

Marlow complained about the tedious, uncomfortable day they had had. They had been told it was but forty miles and they had come above threescore. Hastings, flinging himself into a chair, observed that it all came from Marlow's unaccountable reserve that would not let them inquire more frequently on the way. When Marlow admitted that he was unwilling to lay himself under an obligation to everyone he met, Hastings retorted that at that time, however, they were not likely to receive any answer.

Notes:

(a) Words such as 'complained' and 'retorted' are inserted to convey the tone of the original.
(b) The stage direction is included as being part of the action.
(c) The past tense is usually put one tense further back; 'were' becomes 'had been', etc.
(d) There is, however, no need to change the 'was' in the second sentence.
(e) 'At present' in the last sentence becomes 'at that time'. Similarly 'now' becomes 'next day', 'yesterday' becomes 'the previous day', etc.
(f) To gain better continuity, Marlow's last sentence is made into an adverbial clause by introducing the conjunction 'when'.

All the rules for turning direct speech into indirect speech are given in the notes to the examples above. They can be summarized as follows:

1 All inverted commas come out, and paragraphing and punctuation are arranged to suit normal requirements.
2 All pronouns and possessive adjectives are changed to the third person. (Difficulties often arise when there is more than one 'he' in the passage, but this can usually be avoided by the judicious use of names in place of the pronouns.)
3 All tenses go one further back in time.
4 Adverbs and demonstrative pronouns and adjectives must be changed to fit the new tense (e.g. 'this' becomes 'that', 'today' becomes 'that day', etc.).
5 These rules, of course, work in reverse when indirect speech is being changed into direct speech.

Examination practice

1 Rewrite the following as indirect speech:

'Come here!' John shouted.

William did not respond at once, but then stood up slowly and said: 'All right! I'll come. But there's no need to shout.'

'You must go today,' John said. 'You cannot stay here any longer.'

'I am quite willing to leave here,' William answered. 'Nothing, in fact, would please me better. But could I not go tomorrow? This hasty departure is most inconvenient.'

'No! It must be today. At once!'

'Very well. If this is your order, I must not be held responsible for the consequences.'

'Is that a threat?'

'No, not a threat,' replied William with a smile, 'but if you like, you can take it as a warning.'

2 Rewrite the following as an extract from a novel, using direct speech where necessary:

Mrs Milvain, in her half-absent way, said that what her son, Jasper, had told them was all very sad; and when she asked if it meant that the Reardons could never have a holiday, he replied that it was quite out of the question. She asked if it wouldn't be possible if he invited them to their house for a week, but he said that was quite impossible, and she knew that very well, to which she replied affectionately that they should make the effort.

7 Figures of Speech and Idiom

Nearly all boards include understanding of figurative and idiomatic expressions in the syllabus. This is to be expected, because the English language is very rich in idiom, and you must know when the words are being used literally, figuratively or idiomatically. To put it at its most obvious, when you read the sentence *It was raining cats and dogs*, you must understand that it does not mean that cats and dogs were dropping from the clouds, but that it was raining extremely heavily.

Sometimes separate questions are set, but with many boards the questions on figures of speech and idiom are part of the vocabulary or comprehension test, even when the latter is in a multiple choice form. Usually, you are not asked to name figures of speech, but sometimes the questions imply that you do know some of the terminology. The following question, set by an examining board, is an example:

> *Choose four of the following words, and for each write two sentences in which the word is used (i) literally and (ii) metaphorically.* (AEB)
> *Example: valley*
> (i) *Between the steep hills is a deep valley with streams flowing down it.* (*literal*)
> (ii) *After the death of her husband she lived in a valley of despair, although many friends tried to raise her spirits.* (*metaphorical*)
> chain   ceiling   highway   juggle   knot   sea

The example does, of course, help to explain what is meant by *metaphorically*; but it is not a very pleasant feeling to arrive in the examination room and have something completely new sprung upon you. You are much more likely to tackle such a question with confidence if you know beforehand what a *metaphor* is. You can then be quite sure that you are answering this question correctly. So this chapter includes a list of the most common figures of speech, with examples. They should help you to recognize when, and how, the English language is being used in a special way, and not only for the literal meaning of the words.

Examples of figures of speech

The following list includes only the most common figures of speech, but it is sufficient for English Language examinations.

Alliteration The repetition of consonant sounds, to gain a particular effect. This is more common in verse than prose:

> How to keep – is there . . . nowhere known some,
>> bow or brooch or braid or brace, lace, latch or catch or key
>> to keep
> Back beauty, keep it . . . from vanishing away?

Assonance The repetition of vowel sounds, once again more common in verse than prose:

> And in the stream the long-leaved flowers weep.

Hyperbole A deliberate exaggeration, to make a point forcibly:

> Our swim in the sea made us so hungry we ate a ton of sandwiches.

Litotes The opposite of hyperbole, that is deliberate understatement:

> If you are going to the Lake District, I advise you to take an
> umbrella because it can rain just a little bit up there.

Metaphor An implied comparison, without the use of *like* or *as* (cf. simile). Very common in both verse and prose. The metaphor can be just one word:

> She is the most beautiful daughter, the <u>flower</u> of her family.

But a metaphor can often extend through several sentences:

> When Janet looked at her life, she saw the same sadness everywhere.
> It was *a sun-dried, barren tract, where there was no shadow, and
> where all the waters were bitter*. But she suddenly thought there was
> *one spot* in her memory which seemed to promise her *an untried
> spring, where the waters might be sweet*.

Onomatopoeia The deliberate use of words which echo the sound or movement of the thing being described. More common in verse, but can also appear in prose (see Simile).

> The moan of doves in immemorial elms,
> And murmuring of innumerable bees.

Personification Some non-human thing or abstraction is made to have some human characteristics:

> Hardship is always coming my way; but Pleasure no sooner arrives than it says 'Goodbye!'

Simile Perhaps the most common figure of speech, in both verse and prose, when a direct comparison is made, introduced by the words *like* or *as*:

> He looked down from the deck of the ship: the movement of the crowd on the quayside ran along the jetty like a ripple on the water, like a breath of wind on a field; then all was still again.

(Notice that this is also an example of onomatopoeia, because the rhythm of the words echoes the movement of the crowd.)

When you are asked to give the meaning of an expression where it is being used figuratively in a passage, it is often easier to explain if you understand what figure of speech is being used. For example, here is a question set by the Oxford Local Examinations Board in a comprehension test. The passage was about roads and the English countryside. Here are the relevant sentences from the passage, and the question:

> *Bearing the signs of its age-long human settlements at about every turn, the English countryside is one of the most densely detailed landscapes in the world. The roads of earlier centuries formed a natural complement to this patchwork beauty . . .*
>
> *Explain patchwork.*   (OX)

It is possible, of course, to answer this question satisfactorily without realizing that the word *patchwork* is used as a metaphor, comparing all the little pieces of different colours that make up the English landscape to a piece of patchwork where small pieces of differently coloured materials are sewn together. But you are more likely to find a clearer answer if you do recognize *patchwork* as a metaphor. For example:

Patchwork is small pieces of material sewn together

---

is not a satisfactory answer to this question because it does not explain how the word is used in the passage. A better answer would be:

Patchwork is used as a metaphor comparing all the different coloured shapes of fields, hedges, roads and villages that make up the English landscape, with a piece of patchwork made of different pieces of material.

Idiom is a form of figurative language, in that the words are not being used in their literal sense, but it is different from other figures of speech. These are used by the writer for one particular piece of writing, usually for one occasion only. Idiom has been, and is used by countless numbers of people on countless occasions; it is a figurative expression which has been absorbed into the language and so gone into common use.

There are hundreds of idioms in the English language, and they pose particular problems for foreigners who are learning English. They derive from many different sources: for example, work (*thin edge of the wedge, hit the nail on the head, have an axe to grind* etc.); or sport (*put one's cards on the table, not cricket, have two strings to one's bow* etc.); or food (*take with a pinch of salt, know which side one's bread is buttered, eat humble pie* etc.); or from the experience of ships (*sail near the wind, take the wind out of someone's sails, in the doldrums* etc.).

In fact, idioms have been derived from every field of human activity. They incapsulate the accumulated wisdom of hundreds of years of human experience.

Here is an example of a question on idiom as used in a multiple choice comprehension question. The relevant section from the passage is the following piece of conversation:

'We don't want you, George, to play with us at all,' said Archie.
'Yes, we do,' said Beatrice.
'He drops his aitches like anything.'
'No, E doesn't,' said I, in the heat of the moment.
'There you go,' he cried. 'E, he says, E! E! E!'

This is the question:
We gather from the words 'in the heat of the moment' that George
  A   was easily made to lose his temper
  B   could not bear to be teased
  C   usually tried to speak carefully
  D   was ashamed of his normal speech
  E   quickly regained his good temper

There is no way in which you can answer this question by looking at the literal sense of 'the heat of the moment'. It is only if you recognize it as an idiom, and know that to do something in 'the heat of the moment' means that you do it when your temper has been quickly roused, that you will realize that *A* is the correct answer.

How do you learn idioms? Many of them you pick up without

realizing you are learning them. But if you do, in your reading, come across a phrase which is obviously an idiom, you cannot look it up in a dictionary. For example, if you did not know the idiom 'raining cats and dogs' it would not help to look it up under 'rain', 'cat' or 'dog' in an ordinary dictionary. There are, however, several dictionaries of idioms or proverbs, which do include most of the idioms used in English, and at least one of these dictionaries should be in the reference section of your school or college library, or in your public library. In these dictionaries the idioms are listed under the main image (or images). For example, 'in the heat of the moment' would be listed under 'heat'. When you find an idiom you do not know, you should write it down in your vocabulary book, and then look it up as soon as you can.

Examination practice

1 Complete the question given at the beginning of this chapter, using the words chain, ceiling, highway, juggle, knot *and* sea *(i) literally and (ii) metaphorically.*

2 Rewrite the following conversation, keeping the same sense, but without using idiom.

'I know he was playing to the gallery, but his performance did bring the house down.'

'I wish, though, he didn't blow his own trumpet quite so much; he will never play second fiddle to anyone.'

'I think you've got an axe to grind there; in fact it's a case of the pot calling the kettle black. You'd steal a march on him if you were given half a chance.'

'Well, at the moment I have got my back to the wall, but I'd like the opportunity to take the wind out of his sails.'

'I think you are skating on thin ice. Mind you don't get hoisted with your own petard!'

8 Paraphrase

In many ways paraphrase is similar to summary, but whereas in a summary you have to give the original author's ideas or argument in less words, in a paraphrase you have to give a full rendering, and this can mean that your paraphrase is longer than the original passage. The technique for setting about a paraphrase is the same as that for a summary; that is you must read and re-read the passage until you understand what the writer had to say.

One good way of tackling a paraphrase is to imagine that a foreigner, with a good command of modern English, has asked you the question: 'What, exactly, is the writer saying here? Give me the sense of the passage in your own words.'

Not many boards set separate questions on paraphrase, but they are nearly always included in the comprehension test. All the questions which begin with the words '*In your own words, give the meaning of . . .*' are really exercises in paraphrase, and we have studied some of these in Chapter 4.

Here is a question which is a test of paraphrase:

Rewrite the following in simple and concise English.   (AEB)
A female person of tender years, while being conveyed in an electrically-driven railway train along a section of the permanent way that was in the course of being repaired, became aware of the fact that the conveyance was proceeding at an excessive speed and oscillating in a dangerous manner. Acting with alacrity, she depressed the alarm lever, which effected the halting of the train. Beyond a shadow of doubt the efficacy of her action ensured the avoidance of a calamitous impact.

This is also an exercise in attempting to avoid jargon, cliché and tautology. It demonstrates that effective English can be simple, and need not include long words and important-sounding phrases.

The question could be answered as follows:

A young woman, while travelling in an electric train over a section of the line that was being repaired, noticed that the train was travelling too fast and swaying dangerously. She stopped the train by quickly pressing the alarm lever. Her decisive action undoubtedly prevented a dangerous accident.

When writing a paraphrase, you must aim to keep the same meaning as the original although you change the words. In the passage above, for example, the phrase 'a young woman' means the same as 'a female person of tender years'. But some of the other phrases are not quite so easy. For example, any substitute for the phrase 'acting with alacrity' must bring out the meaning of 'speed', so we use the adverb 'quickly'. But in the phrase 'the efficacy of her action', the meaning to bring out is not 'speed' but 'effectiveness'; so a phrase such as 'her swift action' would not be accurate; 'her decisive action' conveys more accurately the meaning of the original.

Paraphrase is a most difficult thing to do well, but it is a most valuable exercise as a preparation for both language and literature examinations, because it makes extensive demands on understanding and expression.

The following examples will show some of the difficulties and limitations in the writing of a paraphrase.

1 The first passage is from Bacon's *The Advancement of Learning*:

And for the conceit that learning should dispose men to leisure and privateness, and make men slothful; it were a strange thing if that which accustometh the mind to a perpetual motion and agitation should induce slothfulness; whereas contrariwise it may be truly affirmed, that no kind of men love business for itself but those that are learned; for other persons love it for profit, as an hireling, that loves the work for the wages.

This could be paraphrased as:

As for the idea that study makes men lazy and think only of their spare time and entertaining themselves, it would be very odd indeed if that very thing which causes a man to rack his brains and to be always worrying out some problem, caused laziness. On the contrary, however, it could reasonably be argued that it is only people who are interested in knowledge who like work for its own sake. Other people like work only for what they can make out of it; a workman, for example, works not for pleasure, but only for wages.

Notes:
(a) The second passage is slightly longer.
(b) The original has only one sentence; the paraphrase has three.
(c) A modern equivalent has to be found for those words, such as 'conceit' and 'hireling', which do not mean the same thing today as they did in Bacon's time. Even if you did not know these words, their sense could be determined by a close reading.
(d) Some attempt has been made to retain the argumentative tone of the original.

2 With the paraphrase of verse, particularly if it is good verse, much of the 'meaning' which is conveyed by the rhythm, movement and imagery of the words is inevitably lost in a paraphrase. The best that can be attempted is to give the sense in straightforward prose. The next passage is from John Donne's *Third Satyre*:

On a huge hill,
Cragged, and steep, Truth stands, and hee that will
Reach her, about must, and about must goe;
And what the hills suddennes resists, winne so.

This could be paraphrased as:

The true philosophy of life is always almost inaccessible, and anyone who attempts to attain it has to make a constant effort. It is in the act of facing and overcoming the difficulty that a man finds what he is seeking.

Notes:
(a) This paraphrase, as is usual with verse, is longer than the original.
(b) The metaphor of the hill is expressed in non-figurative language.
(c) No attempt has been made to paraphrase the feeling of strain and effort that is conveyed by the rhythm of the verse. 'Constant' is the prose equivalent of 'about must, and about must'.

Examination practice

1 Write a paraphrase of the following passage:
This Emperor useth great familiarity, as well unto all his nobles and subjects, as also unto strangers which serve him, either in his wars, or

in occupations; for his pleasure is that they should dine oftentimes in the year in his presence; and besides that, he is often times abroad, either at one church or another, and walking with his noblemen abroad. And by this means he is not only beloved of his nobles and commons, but had also in great fear and dread through all his dominions, so that no prince in Christendom is more feared of his own than he is, nor yet better beloved.

2 *Write a paraphrase of the following poem:*

Say not the struggle nought availeth,
   The labour and the wounds are vain,
The enemy faints not, nor faileth,
   And as things have been they remain.

If hopes were dupes, fears may be liars;
   It may be, in yon smoke concealed,
Your comrades chase e'en now the fliers,
   And, but for you, possess the field.

For while the tired waves, vainly breaking,
   Seem here no painful inch to gain,
Far back, through creeks and inlets making,
   Comes silent, flooding in, the main.

And not by eastern windows only,
   When daylight comes, comes in the light,
In front, the sun climbs slow, how slowly,
   But westward, look, the land is bright!

                    A. H. Clough (1819–61)

9 Vocabulary

A good vocabulary is a great asset in every part of the examination. In the essay, a good vocabulary enables you to express yourself exactly, vividly and fluently without being lost for words, and without having to repeat weak words and expressions. In the summary, as we have seen in Chapter 2, a good vocabulary is essential: it enables you to sum up a whole concept or a long phrase or clause in one or two apt words. Accurate comprehension is impossible without a good vocabulary, and the passages set usually demand that you know several thousand words beyond what you use in normal everyday conversation.

The best way to acquire a good vocabulary is to read extensively – and make sure you understand every word you read. You must have a good dictionary and you should keep a vocabulary book of your own (a small notebook that will fit in your pocket or bag is best) in which you can jot down any new words with their meanings. This is a painstaking task, but it pays handsome dividends. It is surprising how often you look up a word, learn its meaning, and then keep coming across the same word time and time again: one reason for this is possibly that you had read the word many times before, but it didn't register until you knew its meaning. This implies you had not been understanding accurately previously.

When you look up the words, and write them down, you gradually make them your own: they enter your own vocabulary. People who are interesting speakers, who write vivid and amusing letters, and who seem to have an apt word for every occasion, are always people with a large stock of words. So a good vocabulary is a great asset not only for passing examinations (and not only English Language), but also to enable you to express your personality. You should aim to become fluent and articulate.

Questions on vocabulary can take several forms in the examination.

Even those boards that do not set separate questions specifically on vocabulary, always include them as part of the comprehension test. If you turn back to Chapter 4 and look through the three examples of comprehension tests set by three different boards, you will find that all of them include questions on vocabulary: in the first (p 81) it is question 6; in the second (p 90) question 3; in the third (p 97), question 2. But these are only the direct questions on vocabulary; many of the other questions, for example 1, 4 and 5 on the third passage, are also testing your vocabulary, because you cannot answer these questions if you do not know the meaning of the words.

Separate questions on vocabulary can take several forms. They can be straightforward sentences asking for synonyms of particular words, such as the following:

Rewrite three of the following sentences, substituting your own words for those in italics, without altering the meaning of the sentences:

  1 The host was *apprehensive* of his wife's *tactless* ways.
  2 His *casual* attitude concealed his *timorous* nature.
  3 His *decisive* action was *acclaimed* by everyone.
  4 She answered in the *affirmative* and went on to *enumerate* his good qualities.
  5 The boss's *cryptic* remarks *accounted* for his lack of popularity.

Questions on vocabulary can ask you to use words in sentences which show you know the meaning. Here you must make sure your sentences do illustrate each word and no other. For example, if you were asked to write a sentence to show you knew the meaning of the word tall, you would not write:

    He was a tall man.

'Tall', as used here, to a person who did not know, could mean that the man was short, thin, fat, or anything else. But the sentence:

    He was so tall that he had to stoop when he came through the door

would give a person who did not know the word, a clear notion of its meaning. Of course, the words you are given are not so easy as 'tall', but the technique for using them in sentences is the same.

Sometimes the question on vocabulary can involve pairs of words which are often confused, such pairs as illusion/allusion, moral/morale, personal/personnel, ingenious/ingenuous, human/humane. When you are compiling your vocabulary book, you should pay special attention to words which are similar in sound or spelling, and make sure you can distinguish between them.

Some questions on vocabulary require you to know the meaning of not only words themselves, but also of prefixes. The following question is an example:

Use each of the following prefixes to form a word.
ante   anti   sub   super
Then compose four sentences (one for each word) clearly showing the meaning of each. In forming the words you may use hyphens if you wish.   (AEB)

Prefixes – and suffixes – are explained in Chapter 10 on spelling. When you are building your vocabulary, it is helpful to know not only what the words themselves mean, but also the parts of some words. So *ante* means *before*; *anti* means *against*; *sub* means *under*; and *super* means *over*.

But far more important than preparing for any of these separate questions is the basic necessity to build up your vocabulary for the essay, summary and comprehension. It is here, in the questions for which the highest percentage of marks are given, that a good vocabulary will pay handsome dividends.

Examination practice
1 Write out 50 words, which, in different contexts, could be used instead of 'go' (e.g. wander, saunter, rush). Then pick out the ten words which seem to you the most expressive, and write sentences illustrating their meanings.
2 Repeat the instructions as for Question 1, but for 'say' or 'speak' (e.g. bellow, whisper, shriek).
3 Write a very short story in which some part of the verb 'to get' occurs 20 times. Then, keeping the same sense, rewrite the story substituting a more descriptive or exact word for each 'get'.
4 (a) Write sentences, one for each, which show that you understand the meaning of the following words: perpetual;   reconciliation; unanimous;   inordinate;   malign;   authentic;   phenomenon; elusive;   loquacious;   voracious.
*   (b) Give one word which is opposite in meaning to each of the above.*
5 Write sentences, one for each word, which show the difference in meaning between the following pairs of words: allusion/illusion; contagious/ contiguous; efficient/effective; prescribe/proscribe; urban/urbane.

10 Spelling

The instructions of every board emphasize that spelling is important in every written part of the examination. 'Candidates should pay careful attention to spelling, punctuation and handwriting' is a typical comment. So, if you are a bad speller, you should pay special attention to this area of your written work, because it is so easy to lose marks. The bad speller also faces another disadvantage: if you are doubtful about the spelling of a more vivid or expressive word, you are more likely to fall back on such words as 'get', 'nice', 'go' etc. This means you are then forced to write with a severely limited vocabulary.

So there are good reasons connected with the examination why you should improve your spelling. There is also a more general reason why you should spell correctly: employers, and other people in authority, are always ready to pounce on the unfortunate bad speller. So don't put yourself at a disadvantage.

The English language, as any foreign student who tries to learn it soon finds out, is notorious for the inconsistency of its spelling and pronunciation. Many words which have exactly the same pronunciation are spelt differently, for example: pair, pare, pear; vain, vane, vein; rain, reign, rein; allowed, aloud; bean, been; sail, sale; wait, weight; weather, whether. It would be a useful exercise to collect these pairs of words, and make sure you can distinguish between them in spelling and meaning.

But in spite of the general inconsistency of English spelling, there are some rules and suggestions that can help you to improve your spelling. Here are some of them:

Syllables English words are built up from syllables. Many longer words are easier to spell if you break them down into their syllables rather than try to remember the whole word. One common word that is often misspelt is 'immediately': like most multisyllable words, it is easier to deal with if you break it down into its five syllables: im/med/i/ate/ly.

Prefixes As we saw in Chapter 9, many English words have prefixes, and it sometimes helps with spelling if you remember the meaning of the prefix. For example, in any word which has the meaning of something coming before something else, the prefix is *ante*:

antechamber, antediluvian, antenatal

whereas, where the meaning is that something is against or opposite to something else, the prefix is *anti*:

anticlimax, antidote, antisocial.

So a knowledge of the meanings of prefixes can help your spelling.

This is also useful when you realize you are forming a negative by adding a prefix. You will then see why *dis*/appear has one s, whereas *dis*/satisfied has double s at the beginning; or why *un*/attractive has one n, whereas *un*/necessary and *un*/natural have two.

Suffixes Many English words have suffixes (syllables tacked on at the end), and certain rules apply here too. One of the most common suffixes is *ful*, which is really a shortened form of the word 'full'. So if someone is 'full of care' they could be described as 'careful'. There are many more adjectives like this, such as beautiful, bashful, graceful, hopeful etc., all with one *l* at the end.

But when an adverb is formed from the adjective by adding another suffix *ly*, then these words become carefully, beautifully, bashfully, hopefully etc.

There is an example of another rule about suffixes in the examples above. When a suffix is added to a word which ends in *y*, the *y* is changed to *i*:

beauty, beautiful; jolly, jollily.

(There are, however, some exceptions to this rule, as you will see below.)

Another group of words are those ending in *our* where the *u* is dropped when a suffix is added:

vigour, vigorous; humour, humorous etc.

Other suffixes to notice are those where the suffix begins with the same letter as that which ends the word, so the letter is doubled:

keenness, evenness, usually, soulless etc.

Words ending in -cede, -ceed, and -sede often cause difficulty. Only one word in common use ends in *-sede*:

supersede.

Three words in common use end in -*ceed*:

exceed, proceed (but note procedure), succeed.

All the others end in -*cede*:

accede, concede, intercede, precede.

Also notice those words where the last letter is doubled before the suffix is added:

beginning, jeweller, occurrence, robber, sinning.

This is usually done to keep the sound of the last syllable of the word short. For example, if 'robber' did not have double *b*, it would be pronounced 'rober', which is a different kind of person. But there are a few words, which you should note particularly, where the last syllable is not doubled, even though the sound of the last syllable is kept short:

benefited, paralleled.

As with pronunciation, the rules for suffixes are not entirely consistent. However, when you become aware of the usual practice, and take special note of the exceptions, you are more likely to spell correctly.

Words ending in y The letter *y* causes special difficulties with spelling because it sometimes stays as a *y* and sometimes changes to an *i*.

In the plural of nouns ending in *y*, if the *y* follows a consonant, then the *y* is changed to *i* and *es* is added:

lady, ladies; baby, babies.

When the *y* comes after a vowel, it is not changed, and only *s* is added:

boy, boys; day, days; monkey, monkeys.

The same rule applies to most words ending in *y* when suffixes are added:

enjoy, enjoyment; play, playful.

Whereas –

pretty, prettily; lonely, loneliness; merry, merriment.

However, note that when the suffix *ing* is added, the *y* at the end of the word is retained, otherwise there would be two *i*s together –

carrying, copying.

Verbs ending in y, ie or ye The many common verbs which end in *y*, or *ie*, or *ye*, should be given special attention, because some of them are irregular:

die, died, dying (also tie, lie); dye, dyed, dyeing; play, played, playing (also delay, relay – as in TV programme); pay, paid, paying (also say, lay); try, tried, trying (also dry, deny, copy).

This is not a complete list, but these words do give the main examples.

ie and ei   These combinations of letters are the cause of much confusion. But there are some useful rules:

    When the sound is *e*, *i* comes before *e* except after *c*:

        achieve, believe, brief, grief, thief, yield (exception seize)

whereas –

        ceiling, conceit, conceive, perceive, receive.

    When the sound is *a* or *i*, *e* comes before *i*:

        freight, height, neighbour, reign, vein, weight.

    There are, however, several words which don't fit the rules, and must be learned individually. Here are some of the most common:

        fiery, friend, heir, hierarchy, leisure, pierce, protein, weird.

Noun and verb forms   There are several words in English where the noun form is spelt with a *c*, the verb form with an *s*, and these are frequently misspelt. Some of the most common are:

        advice (noun), advise (verb); licence (noun), license (verb);

        practice (noun), practise (verb).

However, there are also many common words where the noun and verb forms are spelt in the same way:

        notice (noun), notice (verb); rise (noun), rise (verb).

Joined and unjoined words   Confusion often arises with those words which sound as if they are joined together, but which are not:

        a lot (which is confused with the verb allot), all right (although

        alright is now accepted), in between, in spite of.

But there are, as well, many words which are formed by joining two words together:

        into, sometimes, tonight, whenever.

Take special note of which words are joined, and which are not.

Words of special difficulty   There remain many difficult words to which no rules apply. There is no alternative but to learn them, if they give you difficulty, although it is sometimes possible to invent your own mnemonics. (There is a difficult, but useful word: look it up in your dictionary if you don't know what it means.) For example, earlier in this chapter we noticed the difficult word 'supersede'. It comes from the two Latin words *super* and *sedeo*, and means, literally, to sit above somebody. But even if you don't know Latin, you have probably heard the phrase 'sedentary occupation', which is one you do sitting down – and notice, the letters *sede* are in that word too. So now you have a mnemonic to help you remember how to spell 'supersede'.

But the best aid for spelling is a dictionary, and if you haven't one of your own, you should buy one, such as the *Pan (or Heinemann) English Dictionary*. You can then look up the meanings of any word you don't know, and also check the spelling of any word you are doubtful about. You should then write it into your vocabulary book, in a special section for words that you find difficult. It is a waste of time to look up a word, then forget it, and have to look it up again.

Here to finish this chapter is a list of useful words that often cause difficulty with spelling. Get someone to read out the list to you, and see how many you get wrong.

accelerate, accommodation, address, advantageous, bicycle, caricature, character, committee, definite, discreet, ecstasy, eerie, embarrass, exaggerate, exercise, favourite, fortunately, handkerchief, harass, hypocrisy, independence, interrupt, lieutenant, lightning, manoeuvre, minute, necessary, occasion, possession, privilege, procession, queue, relevant, rhythm, satellite, separate, skilful, sincerely, surprise, tongue, tragedy, truly, until, veterinary, which, yacht.

11 Punctuation

Punctuation is taken into consideration in every written part of the examination, and not only in those questions where it is specifically set; and this is justified because the ability to punctuate correctly must be acquired by anyone who hopes to write good English.

Punctuation is a device used by a writer to help his readers understand the meaning of his words by conveying, in print, the tones, inflexions and pauses of the spoken words.

The following punctuation marks are used in English:

1	.	full-stop
2	,	comma
3	;	semi-colon
4	:	colon
5	:—	pointer
6	?	question mark
7	!	exclamation mark
8	' '	or " " inverted commas
9	( )	or [ ] round or square brackets
10	—	dash
11	'	apostrophe
12	-	hyphen

Examples

1 The full-stop: this is used: –

(a) at the end of sentences which are not either questions or exclamations: –

James went to bed.

(b) at the end of a group of words, which, although not a sentence, constitutes a separate entity in some circumstances, such as an address, or in notes: –

London Road,
Watford.

(c) in abbreviations: –

    O.H.M.S. (On Her Majesty's Service)
    Oct. (October)

NB

  (i) Where the last letter of the abbreviated word is given, the full stop is often omitted: –

    Ltd (Limited)

 (ii) In many modern abbreviations using the initial letters, the full stops are often omitted, and sometimes a new word is formed: –

    UNESCO or Unesco (United Nations Educational, Scientific and Cultural Organization)

(d) A short row of full stops (usually three) is used to show that some words have been omitted from a quotation: –

    'Call me Ishmael. Some years ago . . . I thought I would sail about a little and see the watery part of the world.'

This is known as the mark of ellipsis.

2 The comma: this is used: –

(a) to indicate that the sense demands that the reader makes a slight pause: –

    The clocks were altered by Paulson, who is head boy, for a joke.

Without the commas (or the second one) the sense would be different: –

    The clocks were altered by Paulson who is head boy for a joke.

(b) to separate items in a list which is made up of the same parts of speech: –

    I bought some cigarettes, matches, milk, firewood and string.

NB The last two items are usually separated by *and* without the comma, but the comma can be used too.

(c) to enclose words used in apposition: –

    Alexander, Tzar of All the Russias, spoke.

(d) to enclose words used in the vocative case (i.e. people directly addressed): –

    Please, Sir, tell me the answer.

(e) to enclose adjectival and adverbial clauses: –

    Jennifer, who is only five, painted that.
    If you go, you will be punished.

If the sense demands them (as in 2 (a) above) the commas must be there; but otherwise the use of commas here is a matter of style. The modern tendency is to use as few as possible. The best guide is to get the feel of your sentence by reading it to yourself to see if a pause is needed.

(f) to separate the words spoken in direct speech from the rest of the sentence: –

> My father said, 'That is not what I think.'
>
> or 'That is not what I think,' my father said.
>
> or 'That,' my father said, 'is not what I think.'

Mistakes are very common here. Note where the commas are placed, and where capital letters are used.

(g) to enclose interjections: –

> That, by the way, is the truth.
>
> And then, well, he just went away.

(h) after the person addressed at the beginning of a letter: –

> Dear Sir,
>
> > Thank you for . . .

(i) after the expression which is used immediately before the signature at the end of a letter: –

> Yours faithfully,
>
> > G. Forks.

(j) at the end of lines (apart from the last) in addresses: –

> G. F. Pensford, Esq.,
>
> > 53 London Road,
> >
> > > Huntford,
> > >
> > > > Loamshire.

(For full details of the use of commas in letter-writing see Chapter 2.)

3 *The semi-colon:* this is used: –

(a) in lists where the items are long clauses, the items often needing the use of commas within themselves: –

> You should remember these things when you go camping: check that all your gear is in order; see that you are equipped for all weathers; if you are trekking over uninhabited country, take a good supply of food; take a first-aid kit – you never know when it might be needed; and, as far as possible, plan your route.

NB Although *and* is used between the last two items, the semi-colon is retained.

(b) to indicate that the writer wants the reader to pause and consider for a slightly longer time than he would for a comma: –

It is often better to tackle the difficult question rather than the easy one; because the difficult question is likely to draw the best out of you.

(c) to divide a sentence which consists of two balanced statements: –

A man who evades paying his taxes is a bad citizen; but one who pays without thinking why he is paying is equally bad.

The semi-colon is a difficult punctuation mark to use correctly; but it is one which should be studied carefully. It is a most valuable implement for controlling long sentences, and for helping to draw fine distinctions; but like all valuable implements it should be used with care.

4 *The colon:* this is used: –

(a) to divide a sentence where the second half is an explanation or example of the first half: –

The Civil Service became what Pepys strove to make it: a permanent watchdog against corruption.

(b) to introduce a list: –

I want you to buy these things: a new tooth-brush, some soap, toothpaste and some aspirin.

(Compare this with examples 2 (b) and 3 (a) above.)

(c) to introduce a direct statement or quotation: –

This is what he said: 'Go home at once!'

As Keats said:

'Beauty is truth, truth beauty.'

5 *The pointer:* this is used, nowadays usually only in notes, to introduce examples or lists. You can find plenty of examples in this chapter. A pointer could be used instead of the colon in examples 4 (b) and (c) above.

6 *The question mark:* this is used at the end of sentences which are questions: –

What did he say?

'Can you help me?' he asked.

The question mark is commonly omitted by careless candidates.

7 *The exclamation mark:* this is placed after any word, or group of words, which is an exclamation: –

'Run for it!' she screamed.

Interjections are usually followed by an exclamation mark, but never use more than one.

8 *Inverted commas:* these are used: –
(a) to enclose words which are directly spoken: –
'I never knew,' my brother said, 'where he went.'
(b) to enclose words which are direct quotations: –
He recited the Tennyson poem which begins:
'I envy not in any mood . . .'
Shelley said that reviewers were 'a most stupid and malignant race'.
(c) to enclose titles of short poems or magazine articles: –
We read 'Kubla Khan' in class.

NB In print, titles of longer poems, books, magazines, newspapers, plays, operas and paintings are usually in italics.

Note: If preferred, single inverted commas can nowadays be used instead of double, but both must be used when you have inverted commas inside inverted commas: –

'Have you read the article, "Tree Conservation"?' he asked.
or "Have you read the article, 'Tree Conservation'?" he asked.
Take care with the placing of all other punctuation marks when inverted commas are being used. Notice the placing of the question mark in the last example, and the full stop at the end of the second example in 8 (b) as opposed to that in 8 (a).

9 *Brackets:* these are used: –
(a) for separating a parenthesis: –
He thought (so he told me afterwards) that he had won.
(b) for inserting additional information by way of an afterthought or explanation. This can be one word or several sentences: –
Jennifer told Carol that she would keep her (Jennifer's) place.

Note: Square brackets are sometimes used when a bracket is needed inside a bracket.

He thought any attempt at world government (UNO [United Nations Organization] for example) was utopian.
Brackets are used extensively in notes, but they should be avoided as far as possible in normal writing.

10 *Dashes:* these are used: –
(a) for separating a parenthesis: –
'I told – what was his name? – a ferrety-looking boy we used to employ.'
This is the same as brackets, but it is to be preferred where

possible, because it does not visually break into the sentence so abruptly.

(b) to indicate a break in the sense: –

'You've heard about – That's the telephone. Excuse me.'

The mark of ellipsis (. . .) could be used here.

(c) to denote faltering speech: –

'Well – you see – I – no, I can't tell you.'

The dash is easily overworked; it must be used sparingly, and with great care.

11 The apostrophe: this is used: –

(a) in the genitive (possessive) case of nouns: –

This is Jean's book.

NB

(1) If the noun is plural and ends in *s*, the apostrophe goes after the *s*: –

The teacher gave out the girls' books.

(2) If the plural noun does not end in *s*, one is added: –

These are the men's hats.

(3) No apostrophe is used with possessive pronouns or adjectives: –

These are yours.

The dog dropped its bone.

(b) to denote that some letters have been omitted from a word: –

it's (it is), don't (do not), I'm (I am), he'd (he would).

NB won't (would not or will not).

12 The hyphen: this is used: –

(a) to join two or more words to form a compound word: –

dressing-table, mother-in-law.

(b) to divide a word when there is no room to complete it at the end of a line. Words can be divided only at syllable breaks.

Other points

1 Capital letters: these are used for the first letter of: –

(a) the first word of a sentence;

(b) the first word of direct speech: –

He said, 'Go away.'

(c) all proper nouns and adjectives: –

The Indian people of Nairobi speak good English.

(d) the months and days of the week;

(e) the first and all other important words of titles: –
     We heard 'A Young Person's Guide to the Orchestra'.
(f) the interjection *O* and *Oh*, and the pronoun *I*;
(g) all words which refer directly to God: –
     He sent His only-begotten Son.

2 Underlining: Special emphasis can occasionally be given to one word
by underlining: –
     'Are you sure it was <u>fresh</u> rattlesnake venom?'
(*NB* In print the underlined word usually appears in italics.)
This device must be used with the greatest restraint.

3 Paragraphing: The first word of each paragraph should be set in
about one inch from the margin, and all other lines must begin close
to the margin.
     With direct speech it is usual to give a new paragraph to each new
speaker. This keeps the conversation clear without excessive use of
'he said', 'she answered', etc.: –
     'It's done me no good,' he said. 'There's something wrong.'
     'Where's the recipe?'
     He produced it gingerly from his pocket-book.
     'Was the egg addled?' I asked.
     'No. Ought it to have been?'
     'That goes without saying.'

4 The caret: The device, written ʌ, which is used to show something
has been omitted. It is most useful when correcting work: –

     Usual ˻l˼y is often wrongly spelt.

     It is easy ˻to˼ miss out a word.

Examination practice
1 *Write a short story which includes at least one each of all the*
   punctuation marks listed in this chapter.

2 *Rewrite the following, putting in apostrophes as needed:*
   (*a*) *Thats not hers.*
   (*b*) *Its not its ears its hurt, but its eyes.*
   (*c*) *Dont spoil Joans coat.*

   (d) *The boys explanation was that the money wasnt theirs.*
   (e) *Girls shouldnt shout.*
   (f) *Mens hats are cheaper than womens.*

3 *Rewrite the following, giving correct punctuation and paragraphing:*

   I laid down my pen and betty stopped in her needlework without laying it down betty said i how do you manage it either i am very stupid or you are very clever what is it that i manage i dont know returned betty smiling she managed our whole domestic life and wonderfully too but i did not mean that though that made what i did mean more surprising how do you manage betty said i to learn everything that i learn and always to keep up with me i might as well ask you said betty how you manage no because when i come in from the farm anyone can see me studying but you never study betty i suppose i must catch it like a cough said betty quietly and went on with her sewing.

12 Examination Techniques

The aim of this book is to help you to pass the English Language Examination. Everything you will be asked to do has been explained, so you should feel confident that you know what will be expected of you. That is a good start. But your mark will be determined by what you actually write during the short time when you take the examination. There is no sense in knowing what you should do, and then not doing it when you sit in the examination room with the examination paper before you. This final chapter will give you some useful suggestions on how to prepare yourself for the examination day.

English Language is not a subject which you can revise at the last minute. You build up your ability over a long period of time, by constant reading, writing, listening and speaking. But, on the day when you sit your examination, to write a good composition, and to deal confidently with the summary and comprehension questions, you need a clear head. So don't stay up late the night before; go to bed at your usual time, have a good night's sleep, and wake up refreshed. Your revision of English Language should begin about a month before the examination, reading over work you have done before, so you can see the weak points that need correcting, and note the strong points that you might be able to use. Read through your vocabulary book – not too much at a time – revising useful words for the composition and summary, and noting how to spell them correctly. Revise your punctuation, noting the mistakes you commonly make. Are you quite sure, for example, where and how you should use an apostrophe? If not, look it up in the chapter on punctuation in this book. When you go into the examination room you should be refreshed, alert, relaxed and confident, so that you enjoy taking the examination.

When you are told you can begin, don't rush into the questions straightaway. Read all the instructions slowly and carefully to make sure you do exactly what you are asked to do. This takes less than one minute; however, every year, dozens of candidates write more, or less, than they need to do. This advice is also important for every individual question, particularly for those that have more than one part; in the heat of the examination room it is all too easy to overlook, or forget, the second part of a question when you have completed the first part.

Before you set out to write your answers, time yourself carefully and allot your time roughly according to the importance of the questions. Most examination papers state the number of marks given for each question, and this should give you some guide for timing. Don't spend 30 minutes on a question for which 4 marks are allowed, and then rush another question with 20 marks in 5 minutes. Time yourself carefully for the planning, rough work and finished copy stages of the composition and summary. There are no extra marks for finishing early; but neither will you be given any marks for anything not written. The best way to plan your timing is to do, as part of your revision, two or three past papers of your board, timing yourself strictly. You should aim to finish everything, including adequate time to read over and correct your work, within 5 minutes of the time allowed.

Allow yourself time to write clearly and neatly. Try to picture in your mind, now, the examiner as he sits in his study marking a great pile of examination papers. He takes yours off the pile. He is bound to look on it favourably if it is clearly written and neatly laid out. Don't crush everything together, but leave plenty of space so it is easy to mark. Make sure that every answer is numbered, and with exactly the same numbering and lettering as the questions. It is surprising how many candidates fail to number their answers, so the examiner is often unsure exactly which question he is marking. You don't help him either if you number your answers A 1, 2, 3 etc., when the questions are numbered 1 (a), (b), (c) etc.

Finally, when you read over your answers and correct any errors, make sure your corrections are clear and neat. If you need to correct a spelling error, it is usually better to cross out the whole word and write the correction over the top, although the caret, used neatly, is useful for some corrections. Pay special attention with the spelling of words which appear on the examination paper; examiners do not look kindly on candidates who cannot copy out correctly words which appear in the questions. Make sure your punctuation is clear: a splodge on the page that could be a full-stop or comma will be counted as wrong. It is up to you to make everything clear. This is particularly important where you are told to do all your rough work on the examination paper you hand in. Make sure that it is quite clear what is your rough work, and which your finished answers. One neat line through all your rough work is enough to indicate that it is not to be marked.

Most of these suggestions are just plain common sense. Make sure you use it.

Good luck in the examination!

Index

P. J. Hills and H. Barlow
Effective Study Skills £1.95

The contents of this Study Aid include : focusing attention and concentration, reading faster and more efficiently, finding information and using libraries, making notes, essay writing, punctuation and spelling, revision, taking an examination.

A complete guide to effective study, designed to help students eliminate indecision, anxiety and time-wasting and to introduce to them vital but often neglected techniques of study.

C. Beswick and P. J. Downs
French £1.95

The contents of this Study Aid include : revising grammar, revising vocabulary, exam preparation, translation from French, prose composition, comprehension, essay writing, oral tests, dictation, verb tables.

A complete guide to preparing for O level, School Certificate and equivalent examinations in French, written jointly by two teachers and examiners in French.

Brian Catchpole
History 1 : British £1.75

The contents of this Study Aid include : British economic and social history 1700–1980 – the beginnings of industrial change, the first industrial nation, from the First World War to the present day ; British political history 1760—1980.

Together with *History 2 : European*, a complete guide to preparing for O level, School Certificate and equivalent examinations in British and European History.

History 2 : European £1.95

The contents of this Study Aid include : Europe 1789–1914 – the French Revolution and Napoleon, Europe 1815–1849, creation and consolidation of the nation states to *c*. 1870, major themes 1870–1914 ; Europe and world history 1914–1980 – the First World War and the peace treaties, the Russian Revolutions, between the wars, the Second World War, European and world history since 1945.

Reference, language and information

☐ **A Guide to Insurance**	Margaret Allen	£1.95p
☐ **The Story of Language**	C. L. Barber	£1.95p
☐ **North-South**	Brandt Commission	£2.50p
☐ **Test Your IQ**	Butler and Pirie	£1.25p
☐ **Writing English**	D. J. Collinson	£1.50p
☐ **Manifesto**	Francis Cripps et al	£1.95p
☐ **Buying and Selling a House or Flat**	Marjorie Giles	£1.75p
☐ **Save It! The Energy Consumer's Handbook**	Hammond, Newport and Russell	£1.25p
☐ **Mathematics for the Million**	L. Hogben	£1.95p
☐ **Dictionary of Famous Quotations**	Robin Hyman	£2.95p
☐ **Militant Islam**	Godfrey Jansen	£1.50p
☐ **The State of the World Atlas**	Michael Kidron and Ronald Segal	£6.95p
☐ **The War Atlas**	Michael Kidron and Dan Smith	£5.95p
☐ **Practical Statistics**	R. Langley	£1.95p
☐ **How to Study**	H. Maddox	£1.75p
☐ **Your Guide to the Law**	ed. Michael Molyneux	£3.95p
☐ **Common Security**	Palme Commission	£1.95p
☐ **The Modern Crossword Dictionary**	Norman Pulsford	£2.95p
☐ **A Guide to Saving and Investment**	James Rowlatt	£2.50p
☐ **Career Choice**	Audrey Segal	£2.95p
☐ **Logic and its Limits**	Patrick Shaw	£2.95p
☐ **Names for Boys and Girls**	L. Sleigh and C. Johnson	£1.75p
☐ **Straight and Crooked Thinking**	R. H. Thouless	£1.95p
☐ **The Best English**	G. H. Vallins	80p
☐ **First Clue: The A-Z of Finding Out**	Robert Walker	£2.50p
☐ **Money Matters**	Harriet Wilson	£1.25p
☐ **Dictionary of Earth Sciences**		£2.95p
☐ **Dictionary of Economics and Commerce**		£1.50p
☐ **Dictionary of Life Sciences**		£2.95p
☐ **Dictionary of Physical Sciences**		£2.95p
☐ **Harrap's New Pocket French and English Dictionary**		£2.50p
☐ **The Limits to Growth**		£2.50p

☐ **Pan Dictionary of Synonyms and Antonyms**		£1.95p
☐ **Travellers' Multilingual Phrasebook**		£1.95p
☐ **Universal Encyclopaedia of Mathematics**		£2.95p

Literature guides

☐ **An Introduction to Shakespeare and his Contemporaries**	Marguerite Alexander	£2.95p
☐ **An Introduction to Fifty American Poets**	Peter Jones	£1.75p
☐ **An Introduction to Fifty Modern British Plays**	Benedict Nightingale	£2.95p
☐ **An Introduction to Fifty American Novels**	Ian Ousby	£1.95p
☐ **An Introduction to Fifty British Novels 1600–1900**	Gilbert Phelps	£2.50p
☐ **An Introduction to Fifty Modern European Poets**	John Pilling	£2.95p
☐ **An Introduction fo Fifty British Poets 1300–1900**	Michael Schmidt	£1.95p
☐ **An Introduction to Fifty Modern British Poets**		£2.95p
☐ **An Introduction to Fifty European Novels**	Martin Seymour-Smith	£1.95p
☐ **An Introduction to Fifty British Plays 1660–1900**	John Cargill Thompson	£1.95p

All these books are available at your local bookshop or newsagent, or can be ordered direct from the publisher. Indicate the number of copies required and fill in the form below   10

....

Name_____
(Block letters please)

Address_____

Send to CS Department, Pan Books Ltd, PO Box 40, Basingstoke, Hants
Please enclose remittance to the value of the cover price plus:
35p for the first book plus 15p per copy for each additional book ordered
to a maximum charge of £1.25 to cover postage and packing
Applicable only in the UK

While every effort is made to keep prices low, it is sometimes
necessary to increase prices at short notice. Pan Books reserve
the right to show on covers and charge new retail prices which
may differ from those advertised in the text or elsewhere